"In a world where words are often used poorly and harmfully, here is a guide for allowing the very Word of Life to become enfleshed through our lives and in our homes by the grace of God and the power of the Holy Spirit."

—Glenn and Holly Packiam, Colorado Springs, CO

"*Giving Your Words* is full of ways to relate with our children as Jesus did with His disciples. This book will speak to so many parents who love their children but aren't sure how to disciple them."

—Gary and Lynn Custer, Fuquay-Varina, NC

"Sally and Clay give us a fresh reminder of the importance of making words the music and soundtrack to our children's lives, and that good words are like good food: they nourish the body, satisfy the soul, and make us strong for living."

—Jacqui Wakelam, London, UK

"Clay and Sally dig deep into how we are shaped by words, and how as parents we shape and form our children by the words we use."

—Steve and Terri Moon, Colorado Springs, CO

"In *Giving Your Words*, Sally and Clay provide sage parenting guidance that is rooted in Scripture and their years of building a 'verbal home' in their family. If you're a parent, you'll want to grab a cup of coffee and feast on this hope-filled exclamation point on the Clarksons' years of faithful work."

—Chris Stroup, Colorado Springs, CO

"This is encouragement to authentically use your words as parents to nurture your children into mature, godly men and women of character, depth, and intimacy with God."

—David and Margaret Sachsenmaier, Colorado Springs, CO

"This book paints a picture of the possibilities open to us when we embrace the power of words as parents: first, the word of God in our own lives, then the words we speak to our children."

—Misty Krasawski, Franklin, TN

"Through their words, Clay and Sally guide us to see all of life as opportunities to teach, shape, and influence our children's lives with God's goodness, beauty, truth, and love."

—Ben and Anna Holsteen, St Andrews, Scotland

"As a father, I see every day the power and subtlety of verbal interaction with my children. What Clay and Sally have compiled here is a treasure trove not only of their own wisdom, but of the accumulated wisdom of humanity on how we can talk to our children."

—Brian Brown, Colorado Springs, CO

"This book is deeply inspirational, transformative, and yet practical for parents and families."

—Gretchen Roberts, MD, Wilmington, NC

"*Giving Your Words* will help parents at all stages verbally express love and guide their children toward faith in the living God. This is a book for every parent."

—Jennie Nelson, Eagle, ID

GIVING
YOUR
WORDS

The LIFEGIVING POWER

of a VERBAL HOME

for FAMILY FAITH FORMATION

SALLY AND CLAY CLARKSON

BETHANYHOUSE

a division of Baker Publishing Group

Minneapolis, Minnesota

Published by Bethany House Publishers
11400 Hampshire Avenue South
Minneapolis, Minnesota 55438
www.bethanyhouse.com

Bethany House Publishers is a division of
Baker Publishing Group, Grand Rapids, Michigan

Printed in the United States of America

ISBN 978-0-7642-3592-4

Library of Congress Control Number: 2022015492

Cover design by Laura Palma

Published in association with The Bindery Agency, www.TheBinderyAgency.com

22 23 24 25 26 27 28   7 6 5 4 3 2 1

Contents

5

LIFEGIVING WORDS 205

Foreword

Of the many lessons I've learned from Sally and Clay Clarkson over the years, the single most poignant bit of wisdom I've gleaned is this: in a world wrought with worry, aching for Truth, and full of so many things we cannot control, the place where we can make the biggest impact for good is within the four walls of our homes.

What a beautiful, grace-filled concept for a busy, often overwhelmed, perfectionist mama to hear—even and especially as it sits contrary to what our busy, fast-paced world is telling us. There is often so much to do outside our homes that we forget the power we have within them. Home matters on a deeply spiritual and powerful level. It is there that bellies are nourished, spirits are soothed, and hearts are shaped. Home is where we are welcomed with a hug, a warm meal, a place on the sofa, and a listening ear. Home is where we can be truly known, where we can stop pretending and take off the cloaks of whoever we are trying to be outside those walls. Home is a sacred, special, spiritual place.

Giving Your Words digs even deeper into this concept, exploring the power of our words: of stories, questions, truth, encouragement, and so much more. In the pages of this book, we are reminded that while grand achievements and mountains moved are wonderful, it is imperative to turn our eyes toward that which may seem so simple, but is so important: our time spent in conversation with our children.

As a mom to three spunky, spirited children, I have seen the beauty that happens when we make space for bedtime conversations, little hearts pouring out worries as they drift off to sleep. I've experienced the power of a question passed around the dinner table over bowls of spaghetti: "What interests you and makes you curious these days?" Answers pouring out from Triceratops to tea parties to Toni Morrison, hearts ablaze. I've held sweaty pre-teen hands and listened as tender prayers are offered, God's ear bent toward us. From fairy tales to future plans, words have shaped who my own beautiful children are becoming. And it's my hope and prayer that they will take our words with them one day as they leave the nest.

All of Sally and Clay's work, but especially this fantastic book, invites us to slow down, turn our eyes and hearts to God, and pay attention to the power our words have. I often think of the words we share with our children, at any age, as little nuggets of wisdom they carry with them in their proverbial pockets. These words—reminders of their worth, of God's love for them, of our love for them, of what's most important in life—are with them wherever they go, through great experiences and hard ones. They're with them as they make decisions, as they experience hurt, and as they make sense of the world around them. What a beautiful thing to have to carry through the world with you.

To Sally and Clay, thank you for sharing your hearts and experiences with me and so many others. *Giving Your Words* is a treasure of a book that will shape the lives and homes of so many families over the coming years. To the mothers and fathers who have picked up this book: you are doing a good job; keep seeking Truth and keep pouring it out.

With love,
Emily Ley

Preface

SALLY CLARKSON

My mother was not deeply theological, but her simple trust in God was personal and real. I still remember one special Christmas when I was about nine years old. She and I were sitting on the couch by our towering Christmas tree aglow with white lights and colorful, shiny baubles adorning every branch. Sipping our hot chocolates, we sat shoulder to shoulder, taking in the magical moment together.

Out of the blue, she nudged me, looked very solemnly into my eyes, and said, "One thing is important for you to remember the rest of your life."

I sat up straighter, sensing this was a profound moment to her. She said very clearly, "These words have carried me my whole life: 'If God is for you, who can be against you?' Just remember that God is for you, and you will always be able to know there is no circumstance or person who is bigger than Him or stronger than Him. Say it with me: 'If God is for me, who can be against me?'"

And so I did.

Then we sat quietly, enjoying the beauty together. But since that time so many years ago, I have believed that God is on my side. That He is for me. Even as I can see my seventieth year just ahead, those simple words by the apostle Paul (see Romans 8:31)—God's words—have carried me through many life challenges, and will continue to do so.

My mother gave me her words, and they have stayed with me my whole life.

Words are like food to our hearts, minds, and souls. They have the potential to shape destinies, inspire courage, and instill character. Words can express assurance of love, shape our emotional health, and lay foundations of truth that hold us fast our whole lives. Words have the power to pass on a legacy of faith.

Jesus himself was called the Word, or the Message. He was God's Message incarnate, the exact representation of His divine nature. Jesus spoke words of divine truth, and His life affirmed the integrity of His words as He lived them out faithfully. Christ became for us a model of what we wanted to do in giving and living our own messages with our children.

Recently, Clay and I were sitting on our back deck with the sun setting over the Colorado Rocky Mountains and the fire pit dancing with flames as we sipped cool drinks. It was a perfect moment to revisit the landscape of our forty-one years of marriage and thirty-eight years of parenting our four children, now all adults.

As we pondered and remembered together, it was the words that stood out to us. We had spent our lives giving our words to our children, the words of Christ, Scripture, and godly wisdom. We invested in them words that would shape their own life stories. Just as my mother's words had for me, we hoped our words would be a lasting legacy to faithfully carry our children into the darkness of this secular world with their own messages of light.

During the weeks when Clay was giving this book life and poignancy, I was bundled up in an overstuffed chair recovering from hip replacement surgery. Many evenings, we sat together and talked about the messages that we had given to our children, the mornings of devotions when we spoke of God's truth, the family discussions while traveling in the car, and the many daily teachable moments in our home. We recalled all our days of life together as we had shaped our children's sense of virtue and character, given bedtime blessings of peace to their hearts, and shared secret bedroom talks that assured them of our love.

Looking back, it was like a symphony, with our voices as instruments playing notes in all the different ways that we gave our words. The music we gave would become a whole life legacy, given from our hearts to theirs, that they would carry throughout their lives. The music of our lives and words would be continued in the world through them.

Giving words, shaping life messages, building a legacy of unconditional love and wisdom into the hearts, minds, and souls of our children—that all required intentionality, lots of purposeful moments, and a lifetime of speaking life. As parents, we are stewards of the grace of God to the precious ones He has entrusted into our hands.

We offer this book to you as a picture of what is possible in forming faith, hope, and love in the children God has placed in your homes. It will happen as you give them your words. And remember, as you seek to offer your words, that God is for you. He is for you, and with you, as you leave a legacy of faith in your children by giving your words.

Introduction

THE WORDS OF OUR LIVES

It was a generational keeper of a photograph. Every Christmas morning for thirty-something years we had come to The Broadmoor hotel for breakfast and a post-repast session of family photo taking. Winter had not always been so agreeable in Colorado Springs, but December 25, 2018, offered a stunningly beautiful morning of blue sky, bright sun, and crisp air. It was the Christmas of our thirty-eighth year of marriage, appropriately one full generation in the Bible. Our children were grown and living all over the world, and we knew this might be the last time we would all be able to gather this way. The night before, on Christmas Eve, we had enjoyed our traditional Shepherds' Meal of potato soup, fresh herb bread loaf, cheeses, nuts, and fruits, followed by Clay's reading of the nativity story. Christmas morning we had risen early, enjoyed hot chocolate, opened our stockings (a favorite Christmas morning tradition), and then headed off to The Broadmoor for a leisurely breakfast.

13

After a walk around the lake and some candid photos, it was time for the traditional Christmas family photo. We decided to try a new setting, collecting ourselves around a lakeside bench as Nathan posed us—Mom and Dad sitting, kids standing behind us—and Joel set the timer on his iPhone. He hurried back to the bench bunch for the digital countdown, and a moment of memory was captured in a surprisingly good Clarkson family photo. But what was not captured in that Christmas Day image was what has really always defined the Clarkson family—not the visual, but the verbal; not the images, but the words. Truth be told, we probably all wished there was a camera that could take verbalgraphs, capturing all the words of so many spoken moments in our lives. During those ten days together at the family home in Monument, whenever we were all together, it was altogether verbal—in the car, at breakfast in the den, at tea times on the deck, in the evening on the front porch, on long walks, at dinner around the table. Wherever we were, there were words.

As that Christmas Day came to a close, we were all on the backyard deck in a circle of chairs around the new fire pit. With zipped-up winter jackets, lap blankets, hot drinks, and the fire pit flame set to high, we sloughed off the encroaching cool of night as the sun slipped behind the mountains. Another family conversation needed to run its course before we would seek warmth inside. All the kids were sharing memories of growing up in the always verbal and word-driven atmosphere of our home. Listening to them talk, it was clear to us as parents that words had not just filled their lives but formed them, shaping our children into the word-loving adults they had become and were becoming.

They fondly remembered the countless dinner table discussions throughout their childhoods and teens. They recalled Sarah's amazing ability to read and remember books, Joel's penchant for long and insightful explanations of theology, Nathan's challenging questions and opinions about life, and Joy's insistence as the youngest on being heard in family discussions. They talked about a life of reading, and how books and stories had formed their growing minds. They talked about poems and speeches memorized and recited, *Our 24 Family Ways*, birthday breakfasts, prayers and readings, and annual family day mornings of remembering. As the sun set, the cold rose, and the conversation drew to a close, there was a brief "look at us now" moment. They had all become people of words—authors of books, writers of screenplays, crafters of poems, builders of blogs and podcasts, speakers and debaters, performers and actors, post-grad students of imagination, theology, and literature. Finally, the words of that moment slowed to a stop. Everyone knew instinctively it was time to go inside and sit down to a warm meal around one more table of good food and, yes, good words.

Later that night, after we thawed out and our grown-up children had all gone to their respective rooms, we reminisced briefly about our own experience as parents with the words that had so formed our lives as a family. We've been talking about parenting, and talking as parents, for over half our lives. Very early in our marriage, well before children gave us so much more to talk about, we would stay up late thinking out loud together about what kinds of parents we would be, what our home life would be like, and what our children might become. We plotted and prayed about what kind of life to give to them, but as young and intuitive Christian idealists, it was the spiritual kind of life, not "the good life" of things and experiences, that most occupied our minds. And that would mean giving them our words.

Then and Now

That was then, of course, when we realized how much our parenting would be about words; and this is now, forty years later, when all those given words have come alive and are incarnated in the world in our four children. They're all grown up now, and still growing with God, and we thank the Lord that our words (or most of them, anyway) have worked—they've worked *into* our children's lives to shape their minds and souls; worked *for* them to give them faith and wisdom for life; and worked *through* them as they are making their ways and their own marks in the world for God. It all started in the verbal atmosphere of our home, but those words worked only because we intentionally gave them to our children.

Of course, all our words and ideals also became seeds that took root and, in 1994, became Whole Heart Ministries, a family effort to offer biblical help and hope to Christian parents. Since then, in addition to talking *about* and *as* parents, we've also been talking *to* parents in workshops, events, small groups, books, blogs, and podcasts. And now, as we enter the backstretch of that ministry, we're still looking ahead, but we're also gleaning from the past. The simple truths about words that we share in this book are much clearer to us now than they ever could have been in our early days of hazy, idealistic vision-casting as not-yet parents. Many times, parents at our events would take us aside and ask us quietly with a serious frown, "What is the most important thing I can do so my children will follow God?" Somewhere along the way, we realized that the answer to those "What's your secret?" questions was not in any of our clever, compelling, or convicting messages, but was much simpler. It was, in a word, "Words!"

We are all reminded, every day, that we still live in the Information Age that dawned mid-twentieth century with the computer. Cloud-based computing, digital connections, and ubiquitous screens ensure its continued exponential growth. For parents, that reality has translated into an endless electronic stream of how-tos, what-to-dos, and best parental practices. We live with the constant drumbeat of temptation to pick a voice out of all the noise and just parent by someone else's formula. And yet, we also know we are called by Scripture to parent by the power of the Holy Spirit, and there is no formula for that; it is a life of faith. Parenting with faith requires a bigger picture of a Christian home, not just as a place to impart information, but to cultivate faith formation and even personal transformation. Without that, anything we say will rarely rise to being the faith-formed and faith-forming gift that God intended words to be. Which brings us back to that word.

When we looked back to find the answer to the question that parents had asked us, we discovered one constant factor that stood out across all the years of parenting that happened in our home. At every point along the way, we had cultivated by faith what we describe now as a "verbal home." We filled the atmosphere of our home life with words, and our children breathed them in. We were intentional to ensure that we gave words to our children that would fill their spiritual lungs with the lifegiving air of the "grace and truth" of Jesus and the Spirit and word of God. It wasn't really a "secret" of our parenting, but we're confident now that it—the words—was the single most important factor in our parenting.

This book is about how to create a verbal home. After all our messages, media, and books about Christian parenting in over three decades of ministry, it seems fitting that this book can be like an exclamation mark at the end of a long sentence. Because here's the reality we're realizing: Without the verbal factor, even the best and most Christian parenting advice and wisdom we suggest will be like using low-octane gasoline for a high-octane engine. Giving your faith-formed words to your children is filling their tanks with the best fuel you can give them for running the race that God sets before them. This book is not about us putting words in your mouth, but about you putting words in your children. It's about you, by an act of faith, giving them your words and God's words.

Let us be clear, though, how *Giving Your Words* can help you learn the art of creating a verbal home. We did not set out to write a comprehensive exploration and explanation of the verbal task in parenting. Rather, we mean for *Giving Your Words* to be more like a primer—a starting place to find some simple suggestions, tools, and tips to help you become a verbal parent who is "at home with words." It is a framework to build on, not a formula to follow. We cannot tell you all the words you'll need to give to your children, or all the ways that you can give them those words. Our goal is more focused: to convince you of the lifegiving power of a verbal home. What comes next will be up to you.

It might be helpful, then, to know what *Giving Your Words* is *not* about, and then explain what it *is* about. First, although we discuss biblical and practical theological insights, this book is not a theology of words. Also, though we may skim the surface of language studies, this book is not about linguistics. Finally, though we exposit numerous biblical terms and scriptures to learn what God's word says about words, this book is not a Bible study.

Here is what *Giving Your Words* is about. First, this book is about a charge to Christian parents emerging out of our own parenting experience, biblical convictions, and family ministry. We want to light a fire in your heart to give words in your home the priority God intends for them. Second, this book is about encouraging you to *be* a disciple so you can *make* disciples of your children. Paul's words to the Romans about the gospel are no less true when applied in your home to your children: "So faith comes from hearing, and hearing by the word of Christ" (10:17). It is by the words you give to your children—that they hear from you—that they will find faith and become Christ's disciples. Finally, this book is about casting a big-picture vision for the Christian home. It is about understanding the formative influence of a verbal home on the faith, intellect, and imaginations of your children.

Starting the Journey to a Verbal Home

"Education is not the filling of a pail, but the lighting of a fire." That pithy quote about learning is typically, and incorrectly, attributed to nineteenth-century Irish poet W. B. Yeats. The misattributed aphorism is certainly memorable, but the original saying from which it was drawn is more likely from first-century Greek philosopher Plutarch: "For the mind does not require filling like a bottle, but rather, like wood, it only requires kindling to create in it an impulse to think independently and an ardent desire for the truth."[1]

Here is Plutarch's point. The mind is not like a bottle, a neutral container that requires only filling up with words to make it useful. Rather, the mind is more like wood, a solid source of stored potential energy ready to be ignited and released. When kindling is lit beneath a log, those smaller fires become a catalyst that sets the larger piece of wood aflame. That burning mind is what Plutarch describes as the "impulse to think independently" and the "ardent desire for the truth." Though we didn't usually quote Greek philosophy to each other, those were qualities we wanted for our children, and we believed that words would be the kindling to ignite their minds to think and to seek truth. The mind Plutarch described, though, is not the "empty slate" (*tabula rasa*) of Aristotle, but is rather already prepared and ready to respond. It is the same divinely designed "mind" assumed and taught in Scripture—a spiritual faculty of our being that is fueled by words to become fuel for words.

In some ways, this book is like a conversation about the meaning of Plutarch's words, spoken around the same time that Christianity was spreading through the Mediterranean world and beyond. The Gospel authors were recording the words and story of Jesus, the apostle Paul was teaching about the Christian mind, and the other inspired writers were giving shape to the language and truths of Christianity. Their flame-kindled words, starting from a tiny movement in a troubled country and time, would fuel the growth of Christianity like a wildfire, burning its truths into every facet of world history for the next two thousand years, and fueling the growth of Christianity into the largest religion in the history of the world. Words can change the world.

As for the words of this book, we view them not just as information to impart, but as a conversation to start. We want to engage your mind with *our* words so you will engage the minds of your children with *your* words. Perhaps you have seen the 1987 anti-drug television commercial that featured a human brain next to overcooked fried eggs: "This is your brain. . . . This is your brain on drugs."[2] We want to change that image, replacing the fried eggs with a roaring campfire, and say, "This is your mind. This is your mind on words." Words will light and fuel those kinds of fires in the minds of your children.

Here's the simple path we'll follow in *Giving Your Words* to explore how to create a verbal home. Chapter 1 will consider what Scripture says about words. Chapters 2 and 3 ("Living Words") will consider the kinds of words to give, and how you can give them more effectively. Chapters 4 through 9 ("Giving Words") will focus on six specific kinds of words to give. Chapter 10 ("Lifegiving Words") will focus on the call to a verbal home. The epilogue is words from each of our children, and "Our 24 Family Words of Life" is a resource to put *Giving Your Words* into practice.

We all nod and agree with the familiar adage "A picture is worth a thousand words." But we'd like to suggest that an exponential inverse of that truth is even more powerful: "A word is worth ten thousand pictures." Picture what words can do in the hearts, minds, and souls of your children, and then show them by giving them your words.

ONE

In the Beginning
Was the Words

*In the beginning was the Word, and the Word was with
God, and the Word was God.*

John 1:1

The pre-digital-era photograph still stirs delightful memories—smiling young mother holding her bundled newborn
on a sunny day in May, ascending the front porch stairs
into our little girl's new home. It was our second house in
Colorado, a needed upgrade from the small and drafty split-
level with brown siding and a brown backyard, where we
started our marriage. This one was better suited to starting
our family—a cozy two-story blue Cape Cod, with cared-
for landscaping and a greenbelt walking path just beyond
our grassy backyard. Even baby Sarah, just home from the

hospital, would surely smile if she knew the outdoor joys that awaited her.

The following spring was full of the blue skies and temperate weather that Colorado brags about. By then we had a small sandbox in the backyard, close to the picket fence shared with our next-door neighbor. One-year-old Sarah delighted to be outside in her favorite sunny and sandy spot, where she could play and squeal, gesturing excitedly at Buffy, the neighbors' friendly cocker spaniel. It was, of course, also a time when we regularly played the "Mama" and "Papa" name game with her, each of us trying to elicit her first word. So far, though, the only thing elicited was the familiar toddler talk that mimicked our own speaking patterns. No words. Just sounds. Until that day.

Sarah was sitting in the sand, grabbing and throwing handfuls of it into the air with some degree of childish abandon. At that moment, the neighbor opened her back door to let Buffy out into the yard. As soon as the pooch spotted Sarah, she ran straight to the fence, golden fur flying, barking and wagging her whole doggy body. With a gleeful shriek and a wide smile, Sarah animatedly pointed at the dog and loudly spoke her first word . . . "Buppy!"

Wait. What? This was her first word? As new parents, we were momentarily nonplussed by our first child's failure to acknowledge our parental efforts. But we reluctantly conceded that the cute, fluffy puppy dog that gave Sarah such delight was clearly a winning influence, and we gleefully affirmed, "Yes! Buppy. Uh, Buffy. That's right. Buf-fy." We reveled in the magic of her first-word moment, knowing that very soon more words would follow. In fact, *Mama* would quickly win the "best parent" name game, signaling the beginning of a growing verbal stream of new words flowing from her rapidly developing mastery of sounds and meanings. And we knew that it was all much more than a game. We were giving her words and language to shape her life, and she would return them with meaning.

First Words Last

Why do we celebrate a child's first word? Why play the name game, or continuously offer words to an infant or toddler that are met with a blank stare, bemused smile, or even total disregard? We quietly chuckle at our child in the developmental phase recognized onomatopoetically as *babbling*, knowing that it represents the first attempts of our little one to mimic the talking they have seen and heard in others, especially in us as parents. In that precious "baby see, baby do" phase, a child makes early attempts at making the same kinds of sounds as ours, but they're not the same. The mechanics of speech are clearly working, but the meaning of it is not yet clear.

Still, well before sounds become real words, a child can communicate needs, wants, and feelings—pointing, holding up items, pushing things away, smiling, frowning, grimacing, grunting, crying, laughing. And then, at a time and for a reason unknown until it happens, all the incomprehensible practice at speaking and nonverbal communicating will be momentarily disregarded, dots will be connected between that child's mind, muscles, and mouth, and for the first time, a meaningful word will come out. Intelligent speech has begun. A verbal world is created. And it is good.

That long-awaited first word elicits an immediate and often riotous explosion of smiling faces, cheers, hugs, kisses, and laughter from observing adults. So is it any wonder that your child will want to make that all happen again? Make sounds. Watch faces. Get rewarded. What was to your child a few moments before only a new thing to try, now receives such a positive reinforcing response from delighted parents that the impact is undeniable. At such an early stage of neural and physiological development, that positive stimulus might take several seconds to register, but the inevitable impression it will make is indelible, and with it the rules of verbal communication are being learned and internalized.

They are not written rules, and as adults we take them for granted, but for new word-makers they are newly forming revelations. The first rule is quickly learned—*words matter*. It's a world of words, and everyone around seems to like them and use them, so words must matter. But what makes them matter is what they do. The second rule can be considered the verbal equivalent of cause and effect in physics—*words make things happen*. Some will make more things happen than others, but words clearly cause effects. And as more words are learned that make more things happen, a third verbal rule is realized—*words mean things*. It's not enough just to make babbling sounds; it is clear that sounds—*words*—make most things happen, and certain kinds of words make certain kinds of things happen. So, in a nutshell, meaning matters.

Around this same time, your child will also learn that leg muscles can be tested and tried for becoming mobile. Their first step will also get a celebratory parental reaction, with many more words being spoken in response. Mobility is good too, but it's the mental muscle of making words that mean things and that make things happen that will shape the new world opening rapidly to your child. And the more mobile they become in moving about in their expanding world, the more a fourth verbal rule becomes implanted in their brain—*words are everywhere.* No matter where they go, words are there. Though they can't express it yet, they know—words are everywhere because words matter, words mean things, and words make things happen. It's a verbal world.

And therein lies the answer to the question asked earlier: Why do we celebrate a child's first word? It is not because the child has taken a first step toward learning to speak. The ability to form sounds into words—to speak and use language—is innate and instinctual, preconfigured in every child's cognitive, physiological, sensory, psychological, and arguably even spiritual makeup and nature. The primary contribution of parents to that capability is biological, not pedagogical. We celebrate that first word because a properly used word is the first indication of a child's innate desire to communicate verbally. Parents do not need to teach their child *how* to speak—God has taken care of that. Parents do, however, need to teach their child *what* to speak, or how to communicate—that is the challenge and the influence of a verbal home. And that is why we celebrate first words.

The term *image of God* is never strictly defined by Scripture, but many suggest that the ability to speak and use language—to communicate—is part of that image in us. In other words, the eternal nature of the triune God is that of a loving relationship within the Godhead—Father, Son, Holy Spirit—and that is stamped on human nature as God's image: "Then God said, 'Let *Us* make man in *Our* image, according to *Our* likeness. . . .' God created man in His own image, in the image of God He created him; male and female He created them" (Genesis 1:26–27, italics added). *Elohim*, the Creator God of Genesis 1, though translated as a singular noun, is plural in form, suggesting the Godhead. We are created to relate—to God and to one another—because our Creator exists eternally in a divine relationship of perfect love, and we bear God's image.

But even more, God has designed and engineered us—body, mind, spirit—to be relational creatures. For the purpose of this book, the part of that relational design that prompts us to say with the psalmist that we are "fearfully and wonderfully made" is speech and language. British theologian N. T. Wright notes the importance of the relationship between image and words: "One of the most powerful things human beings, God's image-bearers, can do is to speak. Words change things."[1] We cannot deny the importance of our verbal abilities when we recognize that we enter this world equipped in every way to speak and communicate. The only thing missing is the words, and God has provided family for that.

As children learn to speak, they are at first simply practicing how to use their God-given verbal competencies—making sounds with their mouth. However, that raw, natural ability will develop and mature over their first year, combining with other maturing abilities, until a word is spoken, the "first fruit" of a life of relationship with God and other humans. And the primary way they are made to relate is verbally—with meaning that matters and makes things happen. God's world is a verbal world. It's a world of words—given, received, and returned—and your home is where it all begins for your child.

Before exploring how to create a verbal home, though, we want to take an expedited tour of Scripture to make note of its primary language landmarks—a few selected passages from which we can gain insight into how words are woven into the fabric not just of our natural lives, but also of our spiritual lives. There is no doctrine of words articulated directly in God's word, but there are anecdotal and narrative glimpses of God's purpose and plan for words. We hope the few we focus on here will help you think of words as the many-colored verbal threads with which you are weaving a beautiful tapestry in the hearts and minds of your children.

Words Are God's Idea

Since we've been speaking of first words, it seems fitting to begin a biblical exploration of verbal parenting "in the beginning," with the first words of Genesis. We'll simply make some observations to learn what we can about God's nature, the image that we bear, and the kind of world created for us.

Our story as humanity begins in verse 1: "In the beginning God created the heavens and the earth." The earth is described as "formless and desolate . . . and darkness was over the surface of the deep." But with a tingling sense of anticipation, the Spirit of God is hovering over the surface of those waters of chaos and disorder. Then, into the darkness, God speaks: "Let there be light." The sound of verbal light in God's voice momentarily precedes an explosion of visual light in the cosmos. In the words of Augustine, "But, first of all, indeed, light was made by the word of God."[2] God breaks into time and space, not as an incarnated or visible being, but simply as a voice, speaking words that

29

will culminate in the creation of man and woman, made in His image, the pinnacle of His creative acts: "Let Us make man in Our image, according to Our likeness" (1:26). The beginning of creation, and the beginning of humankind, are acts of speech, spoken by God.

We're so accustomed to the opening words of Genesis that we might miss what's actually happening in verse 3. God did not need to say anything. He could've simply envisioned by thought, or even just willed without words, all of creation into existence—one moment nothing and the next everything. God did not need to speak. British theologian and author C. S. Lewis, in *The Magician's Nephew*, imagined Aslan creating the mythical land of Narnia by singing and roaring it into existence: "The deepest, wildest voice they had ever heard was saying: 'Narnia, Narnia, Narnia, awake. Love. Think. Speak. Be walking trees. Be talking beasts. Be divine waters.'"[3] In the same way, the Bible says our existence was created by the voice of God. Not by a sound or a shout, but by words. Into the darkness, Elohim spoke two words in Hebrew, *haya or*. Literally, God said, "Let light be." And the light that was not before, began to exist, because God *spoke* it into being. There was no one there to hear the words, and yet God spoke. Because words mean things and make things happen.

God chose to verbally speak creation and humankind into existence with language we could understand. As the psalmist would later say, "By the word of the LORD the heavens were made" (Psalm 33:6). Words were not for His own benefit, but for ours. He spoke because He intended for us to speak, and for words to be the currency of our communication with Him and with each other. In that sense, speaking everything into existence was a deliberate act of God—He was giving us more than just creation; He was *giving us words*. Those words, or language, are just as much a part of God's created order as light, land, plants, animals, and us.

God's use of words is reflected in the many references to "the word of the LORD." According to *The Encyclopedia of the Bible*, "In the OT the word is the supreme means by which God the Creator makes known both Himself and His will to His creatures. This means that Biblical religion is primarily the religion of the ear rather than the eye."[4] That is, it is primarily verbal. God speaks and we listen to His "word."

The phrase "word of the LORD" occurs for the first time in Scripture just after Abram's meeting with Melchizedek, the mysterious priest of God and king of Salem: "After these things the *word of the LORD* came to Abram in a vision, saying, 'Do not fear, Abram, I am a shield to you; your reward shall be very great'" (Genesis 15:1, italics added). About six hundred years later—having grown from one family, been enslaved and delivered from bondage in Egypt, received the Law on Mount Sinai, wandered in the wilderness for forty years, and now standing across the Jordan from and preparing to enter the Promised Land—a nation of nomadic people called Israel, led by Moses, are about to enjoy Abram's reward, and the "word of the LORD" is clearly in view again.

Moses has gathered the people and reminds them how, forty years earlier, he had received commands from God on the mountain at Sinai, and how he then "was standing between the LORD and you at that time, to declare to you the word of the LORD" (Deuteronomy 5:5). After reading the Ten Commandments, Moses then declares to the people what will become the most important passage in the holy writings for faithful Jews, still recited twice daily for morning and evening prayers. It will later be called the Shema, from the first words in Hebrew in this passage, *Shema Yisra'el*:

> "Hear, O Israel! The LORD is our God, the LORD is one! You shall love the LORD your God with all your heart and with all your soul and with all your might. These words, which I am commanding you today, shall be on your heart. You shall teach them diligently to your sons and shall talk of them when you sit in your house and when you walk by the way and when you lie down and when you rise up."
>
> Deuteronomy 6:4–7

As Israel prepares to enter the Promised Land, Moses reflects God's charge to him in his charge to the families standing before him—the words given to him, that he is giving to them, are to be given to their children.

He tells the Jewish families that "these words . . . shall be on your heart." It's not enough to simply hear the words, but the words must be taken into their hearts. It is how they will obey the first command of the Shema to "love the LORD your God" with all their heart, soul, and being. And it is how they will obey the command that follows to "teach them diligently" to their children. Moses' point is uncomplicated: They cannot teach God's words to their children unless those words are first on their own hearts. Perhaps we should call this the first law of verbal-parent dynamics—you must have God's words in your own heart in order to give your words to your children's hearts.

When Moses charges parents to teach their children diligently, he uses the term *sanan*, which means to "sharpen."

He could have used the more common word for *teach* that God had spoken to him about the children at Sinai (see 4:10), so *sanan* seems a deliberate choice. A child cannot be "whetted" like a knife, and yet the word is used symbolically of a "sharpened tongue" in other occurrences. Perhaps we should simply let the analogy speak to us—that the words parents give to their children should act like a symbolic whetstone to sharpen them for God, not just once but repeatedly.

The primary way to sharpen their children with words was to "talk of them." They were to diligently teach and talk to their children. They were to be verbal parents. The Hebrew word for *talk* is the verbal form of the noun *word* in the phrase "the word of the LORD." In a hyper-literal sense, they were to "word of them" to their children. And to our modern ears, attuned to literal language, we hear Moses saying that should happen at specific places and times. We think, *Let me get my calendar and get those scheduled into my day*, but to Jewish ears attuned to Hebrew parallelism that would use two opposites to express a whole, they heard Moses say it should happen in every place ("when you sit in your home and when you walk by the way") and at every time ("when you lie down and when you rise up"). In other words, there was no place and no time in which they were not to be teaching and talking—giving their words—to their children. It was a picture of verbal parenting.

We've taken time to look at the Shema because it is, arguably, the primary biblical passage for verbal parenting. *Giving your words starts here.* Giving words to your children is not just about information, but also about transformation—what children hear and believe is what will shape their lives. It's about words that shape the heart. Though we are no

33

longer under the Law that Jewish parents were when these words were first spoken, the principles of verbal parenting expressed in the Shema are no less timely and relevant for us as Christian parents today, more than three millennia later. The reality is that this admonition to parents will be repeated in Deuteronomy 11:18–19, remembered six hundred years later in Psalm 78:1–8, recalled in the parental monologue of Proverbs 1–7, reinforced by Jesus (who would've grown up reciting the Shema) in His "What is the great commandment?" teaching (see Matthew 22:36–40), and reflected in Paul's instructions to families in Ephesians 6:1–4.

Christian parents today cannot neglect the importance of the Shema. God has designed us, from the beginning, to give our words, and His word, to our children. The prophet Isaiah said that just as rain and snow accomplish their purposes in God's creation, so will God's word accomplish its purpose. And in the same way, God's words will accomplish the purposes for which He has given them to us, so that we may give our words to others.

God Has Spoken

Throughout the rest of the Old Testament, the "word of the LORD," the "word of God," "your word," "the word," and other similar references all point to God, who gives us His word. The poetic books—particularly Psalms, Proverbs, and Ecclesiastes—often talk about God speaking. However, when we think of God speaking now, we don't mean that He is giving new divine revelation that will become new scriptures in our Bible, but simply that He speaks through the words He has already given, which we now call Scripture.

We believe that God still communicates personally and individually through His Holy Spirit, but when He "speaks" now it is through His preserved written revelation, the Bible.

Nonetheless, understanding the reality of the oral culture of ancient Israel is critical to the concept of verbal parenting, because that is where the idea of "giving your words" was given birth. However, in this age of media, it is easy to lose sight of that foundational verbal and dynamic nature of God's relationship with us as our Creator when we unconsciously rely too much on print, video, image, digital, and online resources to inform our faith and shape our relationship with God. There has been great benefit and blessing in those evolving aspects of our relationship with the "word of God" since the Creator first spoke light into the darkness, but we should also be aware of what has been lost over the millennia. We inadvertently risk falling into a reductionist form of faith that relies too heavily on the visual to the detriment of the verbal. The remedy is not in vilifying or diminishing the visual, but rather in reaffirming and prioritizing the verbal.

Before we move on to the New Testament, a brief peek at Psalm 78, by Asaph, will reaffirm the priority of creating a verbal atmosphere in the home. In the opening verses of his psalm, Asaph recalls the Shema—the giving of the Law when God "commanded our fathers that they should teach [the commandments] to their children" (78:5). He reminds Israelite families that the key to faithful generations is faithful parents who will "tell to the generation to come the praises of the LORD, and His strength and His wondrous works that He has done. . . . That the generation to come might know, even the children yet to be born, that they may arise and tell them to their children" (78:4, 6). In the first eight verses, Asaph uses nine verbs and six nouns related to verbal parenting to emphasize that children should "put their confidence in God and not forget the works of God, but keep His commandments" (78:7). This psalm about faithful parenting is very near the center of our Christian Bible, offering a symbolic reminder that verbal parenting—giving your words—should be at the very heart of your parenting by faith.

Jesus Has Spoken

But now we need to move into the New Testament. After David, things in Israel went downhill quickly—divided kingdom, Assyrian conquest, Babylonian exile, return to the land, and four hundred silent years with no prophet in Israel. Then Jesus was born, God was speaking once again, and the Christian era was inaugurated. But during the four centuries prior to Christ, the world had changed. Thanks to Alexander the Great, Koine (common) Greek was widely spoken. By the time of Jesus, few Jews still spoke Hebrew, often relying instead on a Greek translation of the Hebrew Bible called the Septuagint. Also, the Roman Empire was rapidly expanding and extending its power, connecting nations in ways they had not been before. When Jesus began His public ministry around the age of thirty, He would be speaking into a culture of multiple languages. Most agree that Jesus, though knowledgeable of Hebrew as a rabbi and likely conversant in Koine Greek, primarily spoke in Aramaic, which was the common language of first-century Judea.

Putting aside the question of the language Jesus spoke, though, a more revealing question is about the *words* Jesus spoke—how we have the written record of the four Gospels.

Jesus was articulate and literate, conversing with teachers in the Jerusalem temple at age twelve so those who heard were "amazed at His understanding and His answers" (Luke 2:47), reading from the book of Isaiah in the synagogue in Nazareth to start His ministry (4:16), and writing with His finger in the sand to end a confrontation with Jewish leaders (John 8:3–9). And yet, He left no personally written record of His teachings. Each of the four Gospel accounts was written by a follower of Jesus—Matthew, Mark, Luke, John—and none cites any written source for their content. Though that might seem strange to some, to us it is a Jesus-shaped picture of the verbal power of "giving your words," but only when you understand the nature of His ministry and teaching methods.

Jesus was a rabbi. That was not a formal title, but simply a term of respect for a teacher or master. Jesus was addressed as *Rabbi* twelve times in the Gospels, by His disciples and others, including Nicodemus, a respected Pharisee and Jewish leader. The common mark of a rabbi, or teacher, was disciples who were expected to follow, learn from, and become like their teacher. As Jesus himself taught, "A pupil is not above his teacher; but everyone, after he has been fully trained, will be like his teacher" (Luke 6:40). A rabbi would teach the holy writings of the Hebrew Bible verbally, and his disciples would hear, remember, and recall the rabbi's teachings, stories, and parables. It's one aspect of the oral tradition from which much of Scripture originated.

The public ministry of Jesus lasted only about three years, on a small patch of Middle Eastern land covering only about a hundred miles from north to south, and fifty miles wide. He was just a young itinerant Jewish teacher, one of many in His time, preaching about the kingdom of God to His fellow

Jews of Galilee in the north and Judea and Jerusalem in the south. He fulfilled the role of a biblical prophet, and yet He was more. His miracles would confirm His authority and divinity, but it was His words that would change the world. He claimed to be more than just a messenger from God, but to be the Son of God, and to be one in essence with God (see John 10:30). His words challenged Mosaic Law and temple sacrifices, offering the promise of righteousness and eternal life based on belief rather than behavior, on faith rather than formula, on love rather than legalities. His words, parables, and stories told of a personal God who wants to give us a new life, to enable us to be born again by the Spirit of God to become His children. This was a personal God the world had never known, and He was walking among His creation, talking with them as friends. His words changed the world not just because of what He said, but who He was. No one has given words like the words Jesus gave to us.

At least two decades would pass before the disciples of Jesus would begin writing their stories of the "good message" they had remembered their Rabbi had taught, "that the Christ would suffer and rise again from the dead the third day, and that repentance for forgiveness of sins would be proclaimed in His name to all the nations, beginning from Jerusalem" (Luke 24:46–47). Those Gospel accounts would record the events of Jesus' life and ministry, His teachings and parables. But don't miss the hidden-in-plain-sight message in them for Christian parents—Jesus did not write His own gospel with stylus and papyrus, but with words and people. Jesus wrote His gospel verbally, by giving His words to His disciples.

The use of written documents would increase rapidly after the time of Christ, with a gradual shift from scrolls to codices (books). Jesus, though, relied on the old-school method of oral transmission that also had served Israel for so long. In that way, He was a bridge between old and new—Israel and the church, the Hebrew Bible and the Christian canon, message and movement, verbal and written. The writer of Hebrews suggests that evolution: "God, after He spoke long ago to the fathers in the prophets in many portions and in many ways, in these last days has spoken to us in His Son" (1:1–2).

The New Testament is full of Greek "word" words, hundreds of them, mostly variations of *logos* (word, saying, message), *rhema* (spoken word, statement), and *lego* (say, speak). Many of those words are attributed to Jesus, but He gave us more than only His words; He gave us God's words: "He who does not love Me does not keep *My words*; and the *word* which you hear is *not Mine, but the Father's* who sent Me" (John 14:24, italics added). But Jesus was more than just a word giver; the apostle John opens his Gospel asserting that Jesus was the very Word of God, "the *Logos*," and that He was there "in the beginning," not just with God but as God, who spoke the words "Let there be light" and made us in His image (see Colossians 1:16). In John's words, "In the beginning was the Word, and the Word was with God, and the Word was God. He was in the beginning with God" (John 1:1–2).

John goes on to make sure we know he is saying that Jesus was God incarnate: "And the Word became flesh, and dwelt among us, and we saw His glory, glory as of the only begotten from the Father, full of grace and truth" (John 1:14). But what does it mean that Jesus was the "*Logos*"? The term, which originates in Greek philosophy, is used sparingly to refer to "God's word" as special divine revelation, and only by John in direct reference to Jesus. Though it is uncertain what was behind John's use of *logos*, what is clear is that he opens his Gospel by mirroring the Genesis creation account. He presents Jesus to other Jews not just as a prophet, but as God—the same God they had worshipped from "In the beginning." Similarly, he wanted to present Jesus not just as *giving* the words of God, but as *being* the word of God, the same "word of the LORD" that expressed Yahweh's essence and mind to Jews in the Old Testament.

John mentions *Logos* as the name of Jesus only two times after the preamble to his Gospel—in 1 John 1:1 he calls Him the "Word of Life," and in Revelation 19:13 the "Word of God." For John, the Greek term *Logos* was the bridge between old and new. In his apocalypse, though, John clearly makes the connection: "and His name is called The Word [*Logos*] of God" (Revelation 19:13). In Jewish thought, one's name was one's identity. The angel told Joseph about the child Mary was carrying: "She will bear a Son; and you shall call His name Jesus, for He will save His people from their sins" (Matthew 1:21). The name *Jesus*, derived from *Joshua* in Hebrew, means "Jehovah is salvation." But here, John declares that Jesus' name is also "The Word of God," the full expression of everything that God is.

We Must Speak

Hopefully, we've been able to lay the first few bricks of a foundation on which to build a biblical vision and a practical model for "giving your words" as a parent. Perhaps one final passage from John's Gospel can become a kind of cornerstone for that structure. It's from what is often called the "high priestly prayer" of Jesus, His last words after sharing the Passover meal in the upper room with His disciples on the night He would be betrayed and arrested. The words of His prayer for His disciples are especially relevant:

> "I have manifested Your name to the men whom You gave Me out of the world; they were Yours and You gave them to Me, and *they have kept Your word*. Now they have come to know that everything You have given Me is from You; *for the words which You gave Me I have given to them*; and they received them and truly understood that I came forth from You, and they believed that You sent Me."
>
> John 17:6–8, italics added

Even in the godhead, there is an order of communication that is not just a theological subpoint, but a model for us as followers of Jesus. God gave His words to Jesus; Jesus, as God, gave His words to His disciples; His disciples would give those words to others, "those also who believe in Me through their word" (John 17:20); and on it would go. All those words are given to be received and truly understood for giving ultimate purpose and meaning to our lives because they are from God. And as parents, we give those words to our children for the same reason. Jesus prayed that night for His disciples, but through them also for us as parents.

Jesus' words are eternal. When His disciples asked Him about His return, His response to them is recorded in each of the three synoptic Gospels: "Heaven and earth will pass away, but My words will not pass away" (Matthew 24:35). In other words, a new heaven and a new earth are coming, but the words of Jesus, whether given by Him or by others, will remain. And you may be thinking, *Well, His words may be eternal, but surely mine won't be.* But not so fast. Jesus also had something to say about our words:

> "For the mouth speaks out of that which fills the heart. The good man brings out of his good treasure what is good; and the evil man brings out of his evil treasure what is evil. But I tell you that every careless word that people speak, they shall give an accounting for it in the day of judgment. For by your words you will be justified, and by your words you will be condemned."
>
> Matthew 12:34–37

That's a pretty heavy verse about judgment, but don't let that part distract you from what Jesus says about our words—they will all follow us into eternity, whether to justify us (the good words) or to condemn us (the evil and careless words). Remember, words matter because they mean things and make things happen. And they really are everywhere, in heaven and earth.

We shared a love for the Lord and for ministry when we fell in love, but neither of us came to our marriage with any experience with children. It was a journey into the unknown we would travel together. But as soon as we found out we were going to be parents, we started discussing what it would mean to raise our child for Christ. The first priority we agreed on was to read and talk about Scripture every day with our children. Even before Sarah was old enough to participate, we made a morning family devotional a nonnegotiable start to our day. Breakfast was the time that worked best for us, to make sure that she would hear the word of God being spoken out loud, and words about God being shared personally. As our family grew, the morning devotional became a lively and verbally interactive time of reading, talking, and praying about Scripture. We spoke out of our hearts to our children's hearts the words of God. That word-driven priority never changed.

Giving your words to your children matters, both the words you give and how you give them. So let's talk about how to give living words so Jesus will find us "holding fast the word of life, so that in the day of Christ I will have reason to glory because I did not run in vain nor toil in vain" (Philippians 2:16).

Living
WORDS

TWO

The Words You Say

> *Pleasant words are a honeycomb, sweet to the soul and healing to the bones.*
>
> Proverbs 16:24

When Nathan, our third child, was nineteen, he received a scholarship to study acting at New York Film Academy. It was a giant leap of faith on the journey he was beginning into the world of acting, but also for us on our journey as parents. We were trusting God for Nathan, but we were also understandably trepidatious as we went to New York City to help him settle into a life and culture much different than any place we had lived as a family.

Our first week in NYC, in the blistering concrete heat of August, tested our faith in many ways, even to the point of wondering if going there was a good decision. A previously arranged living situation turned out to be incredibly unacceptable, and Nathan was suddenly a housing orphan with no fallback options. But then God intervened in a truly unexpected and remarkable way, providentially providing an apartment with two older Christian young men, one the son of a couple we knew from our ministry in Texas. We returned to Colorado with a sigh of relief, feeling tentatively confident that God had confirmed the NYC decision.

The next twelve months were a walk of faith, sometimes uphill but always moving forward. We prayed that all we had spoken into Nathan's life up until then would bear fruit and accomplish God's work in him that year. As he studied the acting craft in a very secular community and culture, we were regularly in touch with him, sharing remotely in all the inevitable positives and negatives of his experience. As he turned twenty and his year of life in the Big Apple came to an end, he was still standing with the Lord. In the next decade, he would go on to become a working actor, write screenplays, produce and act in four original faith-shaped films, and eventually move back to NYC.

As parents, we all secretly hold on to the promise of God about His word: "So is my word that goes out from my mouth: It will not return to me empty, but will accomplish what I desire and achieve the purpose for which I sent it" (Isaiah 55:11 NIV). We hope that our words to our children, fleeting and faltering though they may be, yet shaped and informed by our faith in God, will somehow reflect that divine promise. We pray that our parental words will produce spiritual fruit in our children's hearts and minds, and will accomplish, if not all, at least the best of our intentions.

At the end of Nathan's first year in NYC, the road ahead was still just a haze of intuitive imagining by Nathan of where God might take him. Back in Colorado, we talked with him about his experiences at the New York Film Academy and listened as he dreamed and planned for his next steps of faith. As he shared about some of his struggles and temptations in NYC, he said something that made us smile. He was talking about the times—and there were many—when he had to make moral or ethical choices. He said, "I knew what I needed to do, because I kept hearing Mom's voice in my head, and it sounded a lot like God." Our prayer was answered. The words we had given to Nathan over the years had been assimilated into God's promise that His words would not come back empty. They had accomplished their purpose in Nathan's life.

Words Are Works of Heart

Words matter. Not just any words, but especially the ones that move, shape, direct, and inspire us to God's purposes and desires. For the Christian, biblical words of faith, hope, love, grace, truth, goodness, and beauty matter spiritually. In many ways, we are formed by the words that fill us—we become what we think about, say, and believe. One of Solomon's proverbs says, "For as [a man] thinks within himself, so he is" (23:7), or literally, as he "reckons in his soul." The words that fuel and inform that internal reckoning by the inner person are what shape and direct character, conduct, and decisions. In other words, we are what we think. This is why Solomon said to his son,

> My son, pay attention to what I say; turn your ear to my words. Do not let them out of your sight, keep them within your heart; for they are life to those who find them and health

to one's whole body. Above all else, guard your heart, for
everything you do flows from it.

Proverbs 4:20–23 NIV

Solomon, speaking as a parent, tells his son to "keep [my
words] within your heart." The word *keep* in Hebrew suggests not just passively storing them in the heart, but actively
guarding them there as treasures to protect. Why? Because
they are the source of life, not just for the heart but even for
physical health. Solomon again admonishes him to "guard
your heart." Why? Because the boundaries of his child's life
(the word used refers to the boundaries of a piece of land)
will be defined by what comes out of the heart—words in
the heart create boundary markers for the life. Three verses
later he tells his son, "Give careful thought to the paths for
your feet and be steadfast in all your ways" (4:26 NIV). The
words he is giving to his son will put him on the path of life
with God if he considers them carefully and lives by them
faithfully. That is why words matter.

Jesus affirmed this same truth to His followers: "A good
person produces good things from the treasury of a good
heart, and an evil person produces evil things from the treasury of an evil heart. *What you say flows from what is in
your heart*" (Luke 6:45 NLT, italics added). What is in your
heart are words that are a treasury either of good or of evil,
words that will form and direct how you think and live.
Perhaps Jesus was reflecting on Psalm 119:11, "Your word I
have treasured in my heart, that I may not sin against You."
In Psalm 119, "Your word" or "the word" is used forty-two
times in its 176 verses, often associated with verbs such as
keep, treasure, not forget, and *establish.* The longest psalm

50

and longest chapter of the Bible was written to help us remember that God speaks, we listen, and we keep His word in our hearts. When we do, God's word accomplishes what He desires and achieves the purpose for which He spoke it.

Saying What You Mean

This chapter is about the kinds of words you're giving to your children. Though there are dozens of word categories we could dip into, we've chosen only three as examples to get you started. This chapter about "the words you say," and the next one about "saying the words," are in the section called "Living Words." The foundational concepts in these two chapters of what you say and how you say it will make your words come alive for your children. In order to cultivate a verbal atmosphere of faith formation in your home, you need to think intentionally about those two verbal priorities for living words.

First, though, we need to look at the *one* word that is the most important . . . you. Remember our first law of verbal-parent dynamics: In order to give words to your children's hearts, those words must first be on *your* hearts. *You* are the key. In the Shema, God commanded first that His words were to be on the parents' hearts, and then impressed repeatedly on their children. You cannot give to your children's hearts what you do not possess in your own.

But maybe you're thinking, *That was then, in an oral culture when parents had no choice but to teach verbally. But this is now, and my kids get all those Bible and Christian words in videos and online, in workbooks I give to them, and in Sunday school.* While that may be true, relying too heavily on those impersonal, nonverbal substitutes for your parental voice can redirect your children's spirits. By God's design, they are prewired to expect your verbal influence, but when it is absent, their spirits will naturally seek out other voices. If that happens, you lose the opportunity to nourish their spirits by your own verbal influence and instruction. There simply is no adequate substitute for you giving them your words.

The reason your children need your words is simple: Only words that come from the heart can be truly living words, and your heart and your words are what your children most want and need to hear. When you give your child words from your heart, where the Holy Spirit is alive and working in your spirit, you are speaking from your living heart to your child's. Media and workbooks can be helpful, but they have no heart; they can provide information, but that alone will never be a "living" exchange. Jesus told His disciples, "It is the Spirit who gives life . . . the words that I have spoken to you are spirit and are life" (John 6:63). When you give your child words from your spirit, where Christ's Spirit is alive, you are giving them living words.

But there is a catch—the Holy Spirit will need to use *your* words to speak life to your children. If your words are to be living words, they will need to be living in you first, because you are the default source your children will turn to for living words. They can learn from other voices, but all others are subordinate to your own voice. Yours are the first words they will seek out. Metaphorically speaking, your children will naturally come to the well of your spirit expecting to find living water to quench their maturing spiritual thirst.

To keep your well filled up as a parent, you need to become like Mary, the mother of Jesus. She "treasured" (preserved from being lost) all the things about Jesus' birth, "pondering them" (bringing them together) "in her heart" (Luke 2:19). Keeping your spiritual well full of living words is as easy as following the simple example of Mary—listen to and observe what God is doing and saying in your life, preserve those things in your mind, ponder them in your heart. Knowledge of Scripture is good too, but giving your words is not always just about giving biblical information. It is, first and foremost, about passing on your personal understanding about biblical truths and the Christian life—it is God's word, filtered through your life and spirit, by the Holy Spirit, given to your children. It is pondering the kinds of words and truths we suggest in this chapter and in the rest of the book—living and lifegiving words that you have read and heard and treasured in your heart. Those will be living words to give to your children.

Words That Bring Life

But the question remains: What kinds of words do I give to my children? We have no desire to prescribe certain words to answer that question—it's not about formula, but about formation. So rather than prescribe, we want to describe—to try to exemplify the kinds of living words that you can intentionally give to your children. It's not about creating a checklist of words to be sure you've spoken to your children. Rather, it's about creating a verbal atmosphere in your home where living words are breathed in and out as naturally as oxygen. That is how faith formation will happen organically in your family. Helping you create that kind of verbal eco-system in your home is the ultimate purpose of *Giving Your Words*.

Loving Words

Love is, arguably, the *sine qua non* of a meaningful life. The apostle Paul's poetic paean to *agape*, the unconditional love of God, is unrivaled in the annals of words that have shaped our understanding of godly love for one another (see 1 Corinthians 13). Jesus reminded us that the greatest commandments of the Law are to "love the Lord your God" and to "love your neighbor as yourself" (Matthew 22:37, 39), and that the world will know we are His disciples by our "love for one another" (John 13:35). John taught us that we should "love one another, for love is from God," and indeed that "God is love" (1 John 4:7–8). But Paul, by the words he gave to us, helped us understand how the abstract idea of love actually functions in real life by expressing in concrete words what it is and isn't, and what it does and doesn't do. He ends his poem with words most people will recognize: "And now these three remain: faith, hope and love. But the greatest of these is love" (NIV). But why is love the greatest? Because only love will cross the barrier from this temporal life into the eternal. In eternity, we will no longer need faith or hope, but love will remain and abide with us forever. No wonder, then, that love should be at the top of any list of the kinds of words to give to our children.

One of our children needed to hear words of love. This child had been accused of being irresponsible by a supervisor, unconscionably berated and shamed, not just privately but publicly. What was the infraction? Missing a weekly lunch in order to fulfill another responsibility. It was humiliating and unjust, and it had left this child in need of encouragement and love. Sally was in the area, so they met at a hotel, had a nice dinner, took a long evening walk, and talked through the whole incident. There were words shared of our being proud of this child, and how much God loved them. Nothing deep and theological, but personal and biblical. Just a reminder of who they were in God's eyes. The next morning, this child reported that the weight of the incident was lifted. The words Sally gave to this child were enough to remind them that they were accepted and loved by God.

Perhaps the most fundamental and faith-forming truth you can give to your children is that they are loved unconditionally by the God who created them. It's why one of the first verses you can help your children learn will be John 3:16: "For God so loved the world, that He gave His only begotten Son, that whoever believes in Him shall not perish, but have eternal life." Love by a divine being that they cannot see or hear is very abstract for your children, but Scripture will give them words that form how they think about it. (See "Giving Words of Love," part of "Our 24 Family Words of Life" at the end of this book.) To show us what divine love looks like is partly why Jesus, as God, took on flesh—He did so to become Immanuel, "God with us." Other words about Jesus' love can help define an otherwise abstract concept, such as "Just as the Father has loved Me, I have also loved you; abide in My love" (John 15:9) and "Greater love has no one than this, that one lay down his life for his friends" (John 15:13). Talking with more concrete language can help your child put flesh on the words you give them.

Words from Scripture about our love for one another are less abstract because your children will recognize that kind of love from their relationships with you and others. And there is no shortage of concrete love words in Scripture that you can store up in the well of your spirit to give to your children. What you might not think about, though, is how even those simple words about our love for one another can help shape an understanding of important Christian theology later in your child's life, such as understanding that God is love, and that His divine nature and posture toward us is eternally good and loving. When your children begin to grapple with Romans and Galatians as young adults, the words you give them as children about God's love will help them understand Paul's words about the law of love and living in the Spirit.

One other abstract love word to give to your children will become concrete the more they receive it from you in real-life contexts. That word is *charis*, or grace—a gift from God that brings joy, delight, and favor. Theologically, grace is about the law of love: "For the Law was given through Moses; grace and truth were realized through Jesus Christ" (John 1:17) and "For by grace you have been saved through faith; and that not of yourselves, it is the gift of God" (Ephesians 2:8). Grace is about God's loving posture toward us, both in our salvation and our sanctification. Your child will learn about God's grace from your gentle and loving response when they disobey. They will hear God's grace in your words of kindness and forgiveness when they lie or talk back. They will feel it in your loving hug when they are sad or blue. Your actions will provide concrete examples of the love and grace of Jesus. Grace is a word (and a gift) that you should give often to your children.

Believing Words

Believing words can be, well, hard to believe. As adults, when we say *faith*, we know there is more on the receiving end of that one word than we can express in a hundred words— what we believe about God, Jesus, the Spirit, creation, life, the spiritual world, our spirits, the future, eternal destinies, the cross, the resurrection, and so much more. In that one word are things we cannot see, and yet, as Jesus told Thomas, "Blessed are they who did not see, and yet believed" (John 20:29). Much of what that familiar English word evokes is found in the twenty-seven books of the New Testament, where *pistis*, the Greek noun for *faith*, and *pisteuo*, the Greek verb for *believe*, are each used more than 240 times. When we talk about faith and believing with a child, though, the words we say to them will mean much less to their immature understanding, yet hearing those words is no less important to their developing spirits.

Sarah, our first child, went through a time of doubt and uncertainty about God in her tweens and early teens. She was not leaving her faith as much as wondering if it was leaving her. As Sarah shared all of her doubts, Sally simply listened with an open heart before responding, "Sarah, questioning your faith is nothing to be ashamed of. You're asking the same questions that thoughtful people have always asked about faith. I just want you to know that I will believe in God for you right now, as long as you need me to. And I will pray for you." Later, Sarah would tell Sally how thankful she was that she hadn't condemned her unbelief. It was, in fact, her mother's vicarious belief and confidence that carried her forward into faith again. Sally's words of faith helped Sarah find her faith.

57

What John said about his Gospel also seems true of the entire New Testament, that it was written "so that you may believe that Jesus is the Christ, the Son of God; and that believing you may have life in His name" (20:31). Christian faith is uniquely centered on the divine-human birth, life, death, resurrection, and ascension of Christ, and shaped by His work on the cross. When you speak with your children with words of faith and belief, the more you can make it about the person of Jesus, who is God in a human body, the easier it will be for them to understand and engage in believing. You are engaging their imaginations and training them to believe. As Jesus said, "It is [the Scriptures] that testify about Me" (5:39), not the other way around.

Jesus implied much the same principle when responding to His disciples' self-centered bickering about who is greatest in the kingdom of heaven. Jesus brought a young child into their midst and declared they would not even enter the kingdom unless they would humble themselves to become "as this child." Then He said, "And whoever receives one such child in My name receives Me; but whoever causes *one of these little ones who believe in Me* to stumble" might be better off dead (see Matthew 18:1–6, italics added). Though they had no standing under the Jewish Law, Jesus describes children "who believe in Me" using the same verb for belief, *pisteuo*, as would be used of an adult. Not only can children believe in Jesus, but adults can cause a child to "stumble" (*skandalizo*) into sin or unbelief. A child's faith, though immature, is nonetheless a valid and even vital faith. The believing words you say and give to your children will help form and inform their developing faith. Words are the fuel of faith formation.

Many parents, though, practice faith formulation—relying on formulaic methods and materials to indoctrinate their children with Bible knowledge. We always taught that the real goal of Christian parenting should be faith formation—providing an atmosphere and environment in your home in which your child's faith can grow naturally and produce spiritual fruit. Creating a rich and varied verbal atmosphere is one part of a holistic and non-formulaic approach that will result in family faith formation. The words you say and give to your children add to the soil of their hearts in which faith can grow organically. That was the point of Jesus' parable of the sower: "But the seed in the good soil, these are the ones who have heard the word in an honest and good heart, and hold it fast, and bear fruit with perseverance" (Luke 8:15). The "good heart" is the "good soil" in which the seed, which is the word of God, can grow. The more ways that your children hear you talking about faith and believing, the more spiritual organics the soil of their hearts will contain in which their faith can grow and produce fruit.

Hope, a believing word no less important than its companions, *faith* and *love*, is less likely to be a natural part of the believing words you say to your children. Hope is theologically dense with the hope of our calling in Christ, of salvation, of glorification, of eternal life, of heaven, and more. It is inseparably linked with faith: "Now faith is the assurance of things hoped for, the conviction of things not seen" (Hebrews 11:1). Our hope in Christ is an "anchor of the soul" (6:19) and a source of "all joy and peace in believing" (Romans 15:13). It is all these things, yet hope is not on the spiritual radar of most children. Including words and testimonies of hope in your verbal vocabulary will add spiritual organics to the soil of your children's hearts. The words you say and give to them, even if just passively received, will help form and give words to the richness of the hope that God has provided in the words of Scripture and in the person of Christ.

Lasting Words

To wrap up our thoughts about the words you say to your children, we'll consider what can be called "lasting words." You've heard them many times before. In the language of philosophy, they are called transcendentals—the irreducible and interrelated properties of being that are shared by all humans. Medieval Christian theology focused on three transcendentals that are properties of God's being—truth, goodness, and beauty. And because we, and our children, are made in God's image, these are qualities we all desire and pursue. They are ideals to which we aspire simply because we are human.

The point for this brief discussion is that the words you give to your children will ultimately help to shape their understanding of God's nature as true, good, and beautiful. In a deeply fallen world filled with what is false, evil, and ugly, only the conviction that there is a personal God who stands in opposition to those corruptions of His nature will give your children a reason to press forward in life. If they know that God is true, good, and beautiful, they will, like the apostle Paul, have reason to "press on toward the goal for the prize of the upward call of God in Christ Jesus" (Philippians 3:14). That is why these are lasting words.

True is a word of demarcation—either something is true, or it is not. The loving and believing words we just considered are true, but they only scratch the surface of what we believe. From the time our children were very young, we would tell them that they had a treasure chest of truth inside them, and we as parents were filling it up with valuable treasures— wisdom, understanding, knowledge, discernment, and more. We knew we could not prevent all the untrue, empty, and inappropriate words that they might hear, so we purposed to so enrich their lives with words of God's truth that there would be little room for untrue and unworthy words. We always envisioned the words we were giving to our children as going into those treasure chests. There is perhaps no better biblical encouragement for that task than Paul's admonition to the Philippians to "dwell on," or ponder, whatever is true, honorable, right, pure, lovely, reputable, excellent, and praiseworthy (see Philippians 4:8). His words are a reminder that, because the transcendentals are irreducible, those kinds of true words are necessarily also good and beautiful words.

Good is a linguistic ubiquity in English—"Good job"; "I'm good"; "Good riddance"; "It's all good"; "Good looking"; "Good night!" The unfortunate consequence of its overuse can be the dilution of its meaning when heard as a theological term or in a biblical context. God's goodness for some theologians is a core part of His being from which other divine attributes flow, and yet to modern ears "God is good" can easily sound more like a slogan than deep theology. The challenge for parents committed to creating a verbal atmosphere at home is to help their children hear more than just "God is good" when you give them words about the goodness of the Lord, or the goodness of His creation (including us), or the ways that we can value, reveal, and express His goodness with our lives. We tried hard as

61

parents to avoid trivializing the goodness of God, and to give it a bigger canvas in our children's minds than just a dinner blessing or a worship song.

In His parable of the sower, Jesus concludes by telling His disciples that the "good soil" is found in those "who have heard the word in an honest and good heart" (Luke 8:15). To describe that heart, He uses the two most common Greek words that are typically translated "good." The word for "honest" is *kalos*, which can refer to an aesthetic goodness of beauty and praiseworthiness; and the word for "good" is *agathos*, which can refer to an ethical goodness of usefulness or benefit. The key to the parable is about where the good (*kalos*) soil comes from—it is there because that heart has been prepared by breaking the ground, removing the stones, and clearing the weeds (see 8:11–14). The good soil is, literally, a "good and good" heart that has been prepared to value the goodness of God in all its dimensions.

If God is truly good, then everything He creates, says, does, leads, provides, and promises is good. In his first letter to Timothy, Paul affirmed, "For everything created by God is good, and nothing is to be rejected if it is received with gratitude; for it is sanctified by means of the word of God and prayer" (4:4–5). Our desire as a family has never been only to give verbal assent to God's goodness, but to exemplify it in our lives, even to long for it as the Israelites longed to "see the goodness of the LORD in the land of the living" (Psalm 27:13). After all, Paul also reminds us that goodness is a fruit of the Holy Spirit in our lives, and that "the fruit of the Light [in the Lord] consists in all goodness and righteousness and truth" (Ephesians 5:9). As our children heard these kinds of words, their hearts were formed to value God's goodness.

Beauty is a beautiful word. It's our last lasting word, but perhaps the best. We made an effort in our home to value all kinds of beauty—music, artwork, literature, poetry, table settings, candles, flowers, colors, creation, and so much more. We didn't try to define what was beautiful and what was not; rather, we learned to appreciate and cultivate awareness of and appetites for beauty where we found it. We instinctively knew beauty when we experienced it, so appreciating and enjoying it was more important to us than analyzing and defining it. And yet, we also intentionally found ways to talk about beauty that would give our children words to understand and express how and why beauty is a testimony to the beautiful God who created it.

Our focus was on the natural beauty in creation, nature, and art. For instance, to describe a flower as pretty is certainly true, but it's only a small first step to seeing its beauty. To observe and appreciate its colors, structure, symmetry, feel, fragrance, growth, blossoming, place in nature, and ultimately its purpose within creation—why God would design and create that particular flower—is to explore what actually makes a flower beautiful. And it's the same with works of art, such as a piece of music (melody, harmony, instruments, performance, emotion) or a painting (subject, composition, color, style, technique).

We find beauty as we observe and appreciate what it is about specific creative works of art that provide a testimony of God's beauty. Our lives do not depend on beauty, and yet there is what can seem like an extravagant and even reckless beauty all around us. We are drawn to it for life nearly as much as we need food and water. As C. S. Lewis says in *The Weight of Glory*, "We do not want merely to *see* beauty. . . . We want something else which can hardly be put into words—to be united with the beauty we see, to pass into it, to receive it into ourselves, to bathe in it, to become part of it."[1] Beauty exists because it expresses the nature of the eternal God, from whom all beauty originates, and in whom we find life. The "one thing" that the psalmist prays for is to "dwell in the house of the LORD" so he can "behold the beauty of the LORD" (27:4).

We wanted to communicate to our children that beauty is, in some mysterious way, God's currency and language to let us know what He is like—generous, creative, giving, acting, and prolific. There is a mystery to how we know instinctually when something is beautiful. As Solomon said, "[God] has made everything beautiful in its time. He has also set eternity in the human heart; yet no one can fathom what God has done from beginning to end" (Ecclesiastes 3:11 NIV). We are purposely made in the image and likeness of a beautiful God, and His beauty is set within our spirit no less than eternity is set within our heart. We are, as J. R. R. Tolkien would say, "sub-creators"—image-bearing creations who have been given not only a soul with the spiritual breath of life, but a creative spirit in the likeness of God, charged with the innate capacity and ability to create works of aesthetic and functional beauty. When you say words, not just about beauty and beautiful things, but about the beautiful God who made them, you are giving words to your children to hear what God is saying to them. You are releasing them to be beauty-formed sub-creators for Him.

— • —

We've focused on only a very few representative kinds of words you should say to your children—loving, believing, and lasting words. Our goal for this chapter has been simple—to elevate your understanding of the words you say to your children, from a neutral process of communication to a strategic means of spiritual and faith formation. It is in your power to say the kinds of words that will enrich and inflame your child's rapidly developing heart and mind with truth and grace. But as easily and as powerfully as words can build up and inspire to higher thoughts, they can even more rapidly and powerfully tear down and enervate your child's impressionable spirit. Solomon said it simply: "The tongue has the power of life and death, and those who love it will eat its fruit" (Proverbs 18:21 NIV).

There are, of course, many caveats and cautions that could be said here about the words you say as a parent that can bring death instead of life—words of anger, shame, guilt, harshness, criticism, impatience, fear, and many others. There are also words that your children hear you say that are not meant for them but nonetheless they might receive passively from you—judgment, gossip, dishonesty, anger, dissension, unkindness, negativity, and more. The caution should be clear—*all* the words you say that can be heard by your children will become given words, not just the words you want to give. And as James reminds us, "But no one can tame the tongue. . . . From the same mouth come both blessing and cursing" (3:8, 10). But all those other words are a bridge too far for this chapter to explore. They take us back to Jesus' words, that the "mouth speaks from that which fills [the] heart" (Luke 6:45), whether it is good treasure or evil treasure. So let your heart be filled with good treasure, and it will bring forth what is good; it will be the power of life for your children.

When Jesus was preaching in Capernaum early in His ministry, His teachings were too difficult for many of His disciples to accept, and they began to fall away from following Him. He turned to the Twelve and asked, "You do not want to go away also, do you?" To which Simon Peter responded, "Lord, to whom shall we go? You have words of eternal life. We have believed and come to know that You are the Holy One of God" (John 6:68–69). Our hope is that your children will one day be able to say the same about the words you give, and that they will also find life in the Holy One of God because of them. As parents, may we all have children who will be able to say, slightly paraphrasing John Wesley, eighteenth-century Anglican pastor and the founder of Methodism, "I learned more about Christianity from my parents than from all the theologians in England."

Parenting
VERBALOGISTICS

If good words come out of a heart filled with good treasure, as Jesus said, then you need to regularly and intentionally replenish that treasure in your own heart. The reason is simple: You cannot give words to your children if the well of words in your spirit is dry. As a couple, plan a time to discuss and decide on the words you want to be giving to your children. Create a "Words to Give" journal or digital file where you can record notes on words and topics that you can integrate into your life at home. To start, use the three categories mentioned earlier—loving words, believing words, and lasting words. Add other categories that make sense to you, or use "Our 24 Family Words of Life" for ideas. Then, begin to identify words and topics that are meaningful to you as a couple and list them under each category. Next, consider ways that you can fill your spiritual well with scriptures and ideas about them. Finally, consider creative ways to give those words to your children—keep cards with questions you can ask when you're in the car; plan weekly dinner table topics and scriptures to read and discuss; plan a weekly family time around a passage you can act out together and discuss. Avoid lesson-giving by keeping the activity natural and transparent so it's just an organic part of your family life. And remember—the more good treasure you can put into the well of your spirit, the more there will be to draw out when your children come to you for living water. Let your heart overflow with good words.

THREE

Saying the Words

*Like apples of gold in settings of silver is a word spo-
ken in right circumstances.*

Proverbs 25:11

Our family practice of walking and talking probably became habituated during the years we lived in rural central
Texas, when our kids were all thirteen and under. Two hundred acres of mostly level land with roads, water, ravines,
and fields provided many hours of walking time to discuss
life, faith, and everything in between. But it provided more.
With a morning sunrise we could lift our voices and talk
about Jesus being the light of the world. Passing raccoons,
skunks, and armadillos prompted lively discussions about
God's creativity and humor. Bluebonnets and other wild-
flowers reminded us of Jesus' words about God's care for us
in His Sermon on the Mount. Crops and fields gave us pause
to think about the cycles of life, death, and rebirth, or the

readiness of the harvest. Water running over dams and in ravines prompted thoughts of Jesus not just as living water, but as a powerful river of life. Wherever we turned, there was a living illustration, an analogy, or an object lesson just waiting to be explored. And all these years later, many of those lessons still stick in all our memories.

Why do we remember some words but not others? What makes them stick in our minds? Jesus was a master teacher who knew that "the words we say" and "saying the words" are two sides of the same coin. His words are remembered because He knew when to flip that coin to make His words sticky. As an example from the Gospel of Mark, consider just one twenty-four-hour day in Jesus' life leading up to His crucifixion. On the two previous days, Jesus made His triumphal entry into Jerusalem riding on a colt, and then returned to the temple the following day to overturn the moneychangers' tables. The next day is a tour de force of His verbal gifts. Here's a bulleted summary of that day from Mark 11:20–13:37:

- He uses the cursed fig tree as an object lesson about prayer and believing.
- He wins a verbal test with the scribes and Pharisees about His authority.
- He tells a parable about workers in a vineyard who kill the owner's son, in order to convict the religious leaders.
- He uses a coin (denarius) to turn a trick question, asked by Pharisees and Herodians trying to trap Him, back on them.

- He personally answers the legitimate questions of the Sadducees about resurrection, correcting their misunderstanding.
- He responds to a scribe's question about the great commandments, interacting with him and affirming his knowledge.
- He preaches and teaches the people in the temple, probably with passion.
- He turns the "widow's mite" into an anecdotal teaching about giving.
- He responds at length to His disciples' questions about His coming return in judgment.

Jesus didn't just give His followers facts and information they needed to know; He wrapped His words in a variety of verbal styles suited to each situation. George MacDonald (1824–1905), the great Scottish author and poet, said, "Fact is at best but a garment of truth which has ten thousand changes of raiment woven in the same loom."[1] Think about the kinds of raiment woven on the verbal truth loom of Jesus: story, parable, allegory, illustration, anecdote, analogy, simile, narrative, prose, poetry, apocalypse, admonition, object lesson, instruction, persuasion, logic, character study, history, parallelism, and more. And this list doesn't include other traditional rabbinical teaching methods found in the Gospels. Jesus knew that how He said the words was just as important as the words He was saying. As parents cultivating a verbal atmosphere in your home, you can do no better than to emulate Jesus in giving your words to your children.

Meaning What You Say

It doesn't take statistical study and analysis to know that the average amount of time a parent spends in meaningful conversation with their child today is drastically less than it was two thousand years ago. Common sense suggests that the idea of a highly verbal family atmosphere is not the norm for modern experience. It's easy to trace some of the technological reasons for the decline, from the printing press in 1450, to radio, film, TV, personal computers, the internet, the smartphone, streaming media, online gaming, and more. Simply stated, modern life is not verbal family friendly.

In a study called "Screen Time and Children" updated in 2020, the American Academy of Child and Adolescent Psychiatry reported that the average eight- to twelve-year-old spent four to six hours per day on screens, and the average teen up to nine hours ("screens" include smartphones, gaming consoles, TVs, and computers).[2] A recent study out of England found that the average British parent spends only five hours *per week* communicating face-to-face with their children.[3] Troubling stats like these are exacerbated by the impact on twenty-first-century families of increased mobility and multiple outside-the-home activities. The reality is that parents are rapidly losing their place as the primary source of verbal interaction and influence for their children. Children's inner lives are increasingly formed by other voices, many of which parents are unaware of. To regain ground lost to modern culture and reclaim a verbal home will require intentional planning, work, and perseverance. Only you can make that happen.

Strengthening the verbal atmosphere of your home is also about positively influencing mental development and intelligence. The hard drive of your child's brain at birth is not a meaningless binary code jumble of zeros and ones; there is a basic operating system already encoded and ready to use. Your job is to program and optimize that existing system, and one of the best tools you possess to do that is verbal interaction. The result of your efforts, termed "verbal intelligence," is simply words-centered comprehension, reasoning, and speech. According to one study, "Young children who are regularly engaged in conversation by adults may have stronger connections between two developing brain regions critical for language."[4] In other words, there's a lot more going on in your child's brain when you're talking to them than you can see in their faces. Their brains are getting a workout of words!

This chapter is a limited exploration of how your verbal interaction of "saying the words" can fire up your child's linguistic cerebral engines and verbal intelligence. To keep it simple, we'll look at "showing" and "telling" words. We believe it's not only the words themselves, but the kinds of words your children are hearing from you that can exponentially increase their verbal intelligence, as well as form them spiritually for Christ as they grow and mature. Kinds of words matter.

Saying the right kinds of words takes time, though. Dr. Holly Ordway, an educator and author, gets at the heart of this chapter in her insights about the parables of Jesus: "Just as yeast does not instantly make nourishing bread by itself, truth does not transform lives unless and until it is activated, given form and substance, and allowed time to develop."[5] One of Dr. Ordway's areas of expertise is the power and impact of imagination in communicating spiritual realities.

This chapter is about those kinds of words that can act as forming and transforming verbal yeast in your child's mind over time. Learning how to say those showing and telling kinds of words can help to supercharge your child's linguistic development, verbal intelligence, and spiritual growth. Words worth saying are worth saying well.

Saying the Words—Showing

When less time in families is available for verbal interaction, and the verbal atmosphere of the home becomes word starved, the inevitable result is what can be called an RVE— Reductionist Verbal Encounter. In a family culture where children's ears are moving targets because of activities, isolation, earbuds, and other distractions, RVEs take the place of real interactions, reducing words given to short bursts of who to, what to, when to, where to, why to, and how to. Verbal interaction is reduced to brief encounters of functional information exchange, and little more. One antidote to RVEs is to become aware of skills for "showing" your words as a part of your verbal interactions. We'll briefly consider three of them—showing by timing, by voice, and by nonverbal cues. By themselves they will not create change, but they will increase the effectiveness of the words you do say.

Showing by Timing

To repurpose a familiar saying for words, timing is everything. It's not just about knowing when to say something and when not to say it, but it's also about knowing what and what not to say. The Shema suggests that parents should repeatedly teach and talk about God's word with their children wherever they go and whenever they're together. But that "all the time" standard does not in any way rule out the wisdom of being sensitive and aware of place and time issues with children. Proverbs 25:11 pictures good timing: "Like apples of gold in settings of silver is a word spoken in right circumstances." Words become more valuable when timing is taken into consideration.

Timing means always being ready and able to teach and speak to your children about matters of God's truth and wisdom, no matter when or where you are. Of course, that can be as simple as integrating biblical verses and thoughts into everyday conversations and situations. However, we found it also means cultivating a kind of spiritual sixth sense about life experiences that can be turned into teachable moments, object lessons, or personal stories. It can be as simple as studying a flower, or a hummingbird, or the night sky, marveling at God's design in nature and asking how we are designed by God. Or it can be helping a child deal with a friend's unjust anger by explaining the wisdom of Proverbs, such as, "A gentle answer turns away wrath, but a harsh word stirs up anger." And it might include a story from your own childhood, what you did and how it turned out.

But timing in the Shema might also mean being ready for correction or admonition. It's a different kind of timing, but the wisdom of "right circumstances" still applies. We decided early on in our parenting that we would not correct or shame our children in front of others or in public. Rather, we would wait until a time when whatever emotions were in play had dissipated, and we would choose a place of calmness where there were no people or distractions. We might offer tea or a treat and let them know that we wanted to talk with them about what had happened. Those words "spoken in right circumstances" then had more opportunity to reach their heart. There are unlimited other ways that timing will affect how you say the words to your children, and the Spirit is always there to help.

Showing with Your Voice

Studies in the 1970s suggested that interpersonal communication can be as much as 90 percent nonverbal.[6] That is no longer considered a rule, but the principle is still the same—nonverbal communication greatly influences how verbal words are received. A powerful example is Dr. Martin Luther King Jr.'s "I Have a Dream" speech in Washington, DC, in 1963. Watching the filmed footage of Dr. King passionately delivering his message from the platform on the steps of the Lincoln Memorial, it is clear that his nonverbal body language, facial expressions, and especially vocal intonations add power and emotion to his words. In the same way, your voice is your primary tool for "giving your words" to your children. How you express important words you want to say to them, using intonation and emotion in your voice, will tell your children as much as, perhaps sometimes even more than, what you say in words alone.

Louise Seymour Houghton, a regarded Christian author in Victorian England, said, "There is no more deadly enemy to spiritual truth than prosaic literalness."[7] Her point is simple—a lifeless voice can rob words of life. In other words, spiritual truth spoken in a way that is common and routine, without any expression of emotion or beauty, is in danger of arriving in the ears of listeners as dead words. This is why, whenever we read the Bible in our home, we read it not just as words to be heard, but as a message from the God who gave us His word. This is true whether it is Gospel narrative, a parable of Jesus, apostolic instruction, psalms, wisdom, history, prophecy, or quite literally any portion of Scripture. It is an insult to a child's spiritual nature and budding intelligence to read the "living and active" word of God as though it were just words to be heard. It is alive! Use your voice to give your words life.

Showing with Nonverbal Cues

If you've never acted out a Bible story with your children, why not give it a try? If you model enthusiasm and keep it light, your kids will follow your lead. Whenever we acted out a Bible story at home when our children were younger, we were like actors on a stage. That was not difficult for us since for several years when we lived in Texas, our entire family (even newborn Joy as baby Jesus) was involved in "The Promise," a major amphitheater musical production of the life of Christ. We learned that it wasn't enough just to say your lines and act out your role; you had to *show* your lines and *be* your character. So whenever we did family Bible cosplay, such as for the story of David and Goliath, we were all in—Goliath (Clay) looked fierce and menacing, bellowed loudly, and made threatening moves as he challenged David. David (Nathan) was brave, cheekily defiant, and agile as he ran and swung his sling with great confidence. Not surprisingly, we all remember those times as a family.

We share that only to illustrate what you already know—nonverbal communication makes words come alive. Whether you're reading Scripture, telling a story, sharing a childhood memory, teaching a biblical principle, reading a book or article, or telling a joke, how you show the words you're saying with your nonverbal expressions can be the difference between your words being enjoyed and remembered, or just heard and forgotten. Nonverbal communication is simply speaking with your body to show engagement (posture, hands, arms, head) and with your face to show emotion (mouth, brow, eyes). It's how you show your children that you really believe the words you're saying. For some it's natural; for others not so much. But it's a communication skill that can easily be learned and practiced. So show your children, nonverbally, that you can do that.

Saying the Words—Telling

The second way to overcome the encroachment of RVEs in your family is to learn the art of "telling" your words—using language wisely and well. Considering the diminished role of verbal interactions in modern home culture, learning even just a few new telling skills can be transforming. Admittedly, the skill of telling demands more learning and practice to master, but it also promises to help you become a more effective word-giving parent.

Pioneering psychologist and educator G. Stanley Hall (1844–1924) said, "Stories are the natural soul-food for children, their native air and vital breath; but our children are too often either story-starved or charged with ill-chosen or ill-adapted twaddle-tales."[8] To restate his quote for this chapter: Words are the natural spirit-food of children, the air that they long to breathe; but the verbal atmosphere of home is too often word-deprived or filled with un-telling words that cannot satisfy. As parents, it is in your power alone to ensure that your home is enriched by your words, and even more by how you say your words. Learning just a few of the word-telling arts will give you that enrichment power. We'll look at four categories of telling—conversation, narration, illustration, and integration.

Telling with Conversation

Conversation is just talking. If you're extroverted, you talk more than you listen; if you're introverted, you listen more than you talk; but in either case, you talk. However, the issue is not *that* you talk, but *how* you talk. We all do the former; not all think much about the latter. The problem in most homes is not the quantity of words, but the quality. If we are not intentional in thinking about how we converse with our children, no quantity of words will ever add up to a quality of words. We'd like to suggest a few conversational skills that can add quality to your verbal interactions with your children.

Dialogue is simply the process of verbally interacting with your child; that is, having a conversation. You may think dialogue is not really a skill that needs to be learned, but after thirty years of home and parenting ministry, we know better. You may converse easily with your children, but Christian family verbal culture can still be constantly impacted by inescapable RVE talk, ubiquitous screens, conflicting activities, digital interruptions from mobile phones, and the rapidly shrinking windows of free and easy time for the casual, unhurried talking that every child needs. Learning to be intentional and strategic about simply having meaningful conversations with your child is arguably "Job 1" on the hierarchy of skills for giving your words to your children. If you don't get this one right, none of what follows will be right.

As a homeschooling family, admittedly we had more time for conversation, yet we were not immune to competing influences, so we still needed to be intentional with our time. We always reserved certain times during the day for directed discussions—family devotionals, breakfast, driving in the car, and especially dinner at the table. We would come to those times with a planned agenda of some kind for what to discuss, if only to avoid dead air or meaningless chatter. It was up to us, not our children, to turn empty talk times into meaningful conversation. Our children all had strong opinions, so our typical dinner table discussions rarely needed to be primed, yet almost always they needed to be directed. The topics of conversation matured as our children aged, so by their teen years our table talk was quite lively and sometimes intense. That would not have happened without several thousand hours of prior directed discussions at the dinner table.

We also made sure to include talking times on special days and holidays throughout the year. Our Christmas Eve Shepherds' Meal always included a reading of Luke 2 and discussion of the birth of Jesus, and Easter and Thanksgiving included similar table talk. Birthday breakfasts included everyone sharing a positive affirmation or encouragement about that child's life and qualities. Our annual Family Day included remembering how God had been faithful to us the year before and praying about the year ahead. We did our best to make the most of every opportunity we had for talking with our children.

One effective way to ensure that conversation moves beyond the functional and into the formational is to learn the skill of asking questions. You may think that you already know how to do this, but there is an art to asking *good* questions. A thoughtfully formed question can generate stimulating conversation; a poorly formed one might elicit only awkward silence, an uncertain response, or just a hopeful is-that-the-right-answer look. Above all, a well-crafted question should be an invitation, not an investigation or interrogation. If invited properly, your children will gladly engage.

The first filters to keep in mind when forming questions are relevance and focus. By relevance, we mean asking questions about what is already on your child's mind—a book, a movie, a subject of interest, a news event, a personal accomplishment, a challenge, a relationship, music they like, a goal they are working toward. By focus, we mean asking questions that don't stray down random rabbit trails. When refocusing, be careful to keep it about clarification and elaboration, not slipping into unintentional interrogation. Use open-ended questions that ask for thoughts, opinions, feelings, and impressions, not just for answers. The complexity of the question will, of course, vary according to the ages of your children, but for roughly ages four to fourteen, here are some tips for forming good questions.

Good questions *should* be

- Simple—Ask for one thing with clear and precise words. You should not ask a question in such a way that it is asking for several responses.
- Short—Keep your question concise with a minimum of elaboration. You should not need to go into detail to explain your question.
- Sweet—Always ask invitingly and gently, without any sense of challenge or suggestion. Ask with the tone with which you would want to be asked.

- Strategic—Know what you want your question to accomplish. This is not to manipulate the response, but simply to encourage a good answer.
- Stimulating—Ask a question that you know your child will enjoy thinking about. Affirm and engage their personality-type preferences.

Good questions should *not* be

- Closed—Don't ask a question answerable only with yes, no, maybe, I don't know, silence, or an either-or response.
- Loaded—Your question shouldn't have a hidden agenda, such as to admonish, correct, or bring up an issue.
- Rhetorical—Avoid a theoretical or abstract question that a child cannot easily answer.
- Confusing—Don't ask a question that is morally or ethically vague, or that allows for relativistic values or beliefs.[9]

Telling with Narration

On a macro scale, it is the stories—the narrated histories of people, ideas, and events—that have always been the sinew that held together the bones of cultures, people groups, and nations. On a micro scale, that is true for families and communities as well. In the Clarkson family, our history and culture have been narrated through our own stories. Our children are who they are, in part, because they have been formed and informed not just by their own individual experiences, but also by how our narrations of our family stories have been imprinted on their memories and souls. Identity is inseparable from the narrations that shape all of us, and being a Clarkson is a thing none of us can deny. Telling by narration is another powerful and formative way we can say the words we want to give to our children.

In the early 1990s, we moved from Nashville to family property in rural central Texas, two miles from stoplight-free Walnut Springs, population 708, and thirty miles from acceptable shopping and eating out. We built on to Nana Clarkson's home, and the boys (five and seven) were in the finished half of the attic, across the one-person-wide stair landing from the ominously dark unfinished half. That was spooky enough, but there were also bugs. And the boys were especially spooked by the spiders. So one sleepless, spidery night, Sally reminded them of the story of Joshua and how, when he had to step into Moses' very large sandals, God encouraged him: "Be strong and courageous! Do not tremble or be dismayed, for the LORD your God is with you wherever you go" (Joshua 1:9). Then they sang a song Clay had written for the verse and bravely went to sleep. Two nights later, we all were taking shelter in a sunken tub on the first floor as a dark and threatening Texas twister cloud passed directly over our house. In the midst of all our anxiety, seven-year-old Joel stood up in the tub, raised his fist, and defiantly and confidently shouted out the verse from Joshua. And in that moment of now narrative history, another Clarkson family story was forever imprinted on all our spirits.

You don't have to be a trained storyteller to narrate the stories of your family to your children. You need only to remember and retell them. But maybe you're thinking, "Yeah, but why narrate to my kids what they experienced themselves? What's the point?" The point is that they are hearing the words of those stories from *you*—it is *your* voice and *your* words that will imprint in their memories. It is the very essence of what "giving your words" is all about. When you tell the stories, you can emphasize parts that your maturity enables you to understand are more important or more meaningful. You can subtly add parental commentary that emphasizes a child's character, ability, or talents. You can include personal, family, and historical context a child would not know. You can take what might otherwise be just random facts and details about an incident, and with some imagination, creative word choice, and dramatic narration, turn it into a family story with formative power and generational reach. Just like the ancient Jews, you'll be using oral tradition to form the spirits of the micro nation that is your family.

Many books have been written on family storytelling, and all we can do here is encourage you to explore it further on your own, but there's no better way to give your words to your children, and to their children. Here are a few more general hints to get you started.

- Use basic story structure. Whether you are telling a real story, an imaginary story, or both, (1) start with a beginning, (2) build through a succession of events, (3) reach a climax to the story, and (4) conclude with an ending.
- Use verbs for action. Nouns are naming elements in a story, but verbs tell the action and move the story

forward. Use adjectives (they describe nouns) generously; use adverbs (they modify verbs) sparingly.

- Personalize your stories. Family stories are inherently personal, but be sure to add descriptive narrative to flesh out each family member, especially children—appearance, character, feelings, decisions, likes, values, faith, and so on.

- Tell your own stories. Events from your own childhood can be especially effective for family storytelling, illustrating a point, or illuminating a lesson. Include stories about parents, siblings, grandparents, and other family and friends as children.[10]

Telling with Illustration

Most of us have heard hundreds of sermons, and though we might not always remember the teaching points, we often do remember the illustrations—word pictures, comparisons, object lessons, anecdotes. Your children are no different. The words that will stay with them will not be abstract propositional statements of fact, but the ones that help them picture something concrete in their mind, something they can relate to and understand. For example, salvation is an important spiritual truth, but it's abstract. However, a life preserver when you're drowning is concrete. The gospel is abstract, but a hand holding a newspaper with the headline "Saved!" is concrete. And though illustration is especially helpful for spiritual truths, learning to speak in images about all of life will enrich not only your child's imagination, but yours as well. Brian Godawa, in his book *Word Pictures*, catches that glowing truth like a firefly in a jar: "Our Western bias toward rational discourse can too easily blind us to the biblical power of story and word pictures to embody truth."[11] You can embody truth for your children in the same way that the invisible God embodied the truth of His nature for us, taking on human flesh so we could see what He is like. You can put flesh on your words so your children can "see" in their minds what you want them to know and believe. Your words can create images of truth that will enliven their imaginations to enable them to believe more than just propositions and facts, but to spiritually "see" unseen persons, beings, and realities. All of Scripture is a testimony to us of the power of story, image, symbol, metaphor, analogy—illustrative language that enables us to know and understand the God who made us and the life He made for us.

The Old Testament is full of that illustrative language of every kind. Hebrew is based largely on concrete images, not abstract notions, and even the letters of the Hebrew alphabet are based on forms that represent physical realties—animals, objects, body parts, places. We understand God's nature and His plan for us, because His created order is analogical—we know what "God the Father" means because we have fathers; we know what a "child of God" is because we are children; we know what "born again" means because we are all born. The poetry and prophecy of the Old Testament is full of illustrative language about God, creation, life, love, relationships, good, evil, and more.

In the more abstract and rationalistic Greek language, we would generally expect to find more propositional and prescriptive truth. And yet, the New Testament teems with illustrative language. Unquestionably, Jesus should be our model for giving illustrative words to our children. Though

He did not invent the parable (it was a common rabbinical pedagogy), Jesus perfected its form. What He taught in the Sermon on the Mount and the Upper Room Discourse are powerful words we remember, but His most memorable teaching method was the use of illustrative parables, stories, and anecdotes—the prodigal son, the widow's mite, the lost sheep, the mustard seed, the good Samaritan. And His use of analogy is no less memorable—Lamb of God, Light of the World, bread of life, true vine, the Good Shepherd, and so many more. The apostle Paul and other epistle writers, as they developed the theology of the new church, also used illustrative word pictures such as the body, the armor of God, soldiers, slaves, and athletes. We've just scratched the surface of illustrative language in Scripture, but hopefully you get the picture.

Like all the other telling skills, using illustrative language must be learned and practiced. The easiest place to start is with Scripture itself, waiting for opportune moments in your days to give the words of biblical illustrations, stories, parables, and analogies to your children. But the real fun and reward is when you become the illustrator—finding your own analogy about a journey with friends to help a child understand the Christian life; making up your own parable about keeping a candle burning to encourage responsibility and faithfulness; creating an allegory about the land of faith for a bedtime story about living for Jesus; using a pot of tea to illustrate how maturity takes time and heat; coming up with a simile about the night sky being like a beach where every grain of sand is a star.

It seems appropriate that language itself is illustrative: letters are symbols of sounds, words are mini analogies, sentences are pictures, and paragraphs are stories. Perhaps it's just a reminder that the reason we have the capability of language is not just to communicate information, but to illustrate formation—language is the means by which we are formed as humans, the fuel by which we grow, become, believe, and change the world.

Telling by Integration

The final telling skill is not about how you can use words, but about words you can use. For thirty years, we have championed the role of Scripture, literature, and poetry as formative influences in a child's spiritual and intellectual development (see Sally's book *Awaking Wonder*). Even though technically they are not your words, the telling words we want to close with are ways for you to give words to your children that have formative value because of their form, structure, beauty, and depth. We'll call them formed readings. Though the focus of this book is on giving *your* words, these can still be part of that verbal act because they are given with your voice and integrated into your life at home.

There are any number of formed readings that can be read or spoken aloud, or even sung if that suits you. They should never replace the personal verbal interactions we are encouraging for creating a verbal home, but they can supplement them. There is great value for your children in hearing well-crafted language and vocabulary, yet the most formative part of an integrated formed reading is the verbal interaction it stimulates about what has been heard. It's not just about integration into your home life, but also integration into your child's life. Below are just a few suggested readings to integrate into your verbal plans for giving your words.

- Bible and Stories—*The Jesus Storybook Bible* (Sally Lloyd-Jones); *The Child's Story Bible* (Catherine F. Vos); *NIV Psalms and Proverbs* (Zondervan)
- Literature and Prose—THE CHRONICLES OF NARNIA and *The Screwtape Letters* (C. S. Lewis); *The Pilgrim's Progress* (John Bunyan); *Little Pilgrim's Progress* (Helen L. Taylor, illustrated by Joe Sutphin)
- Poetry and Verse—*David's Crown: Sounding the Psalms* and *Sounding the Seasons* (Malcolm Guite); *Favorite Poems Old and New* (Helen Ferris Tibbets, ed.); a favorite hymnal
- Prayers and Liturgies—*Our 24 Family Ways* (Clay Clarkson); *Every Moment Holy*, Volume 1 (Douglas McKelvey); *To Light Their Way* (Kayla Craig)

— • —

Moses said, "So teach us to number our days, that we may present to You a heart of wisdom" (Psalm 90:12). Over a millennium later, the apostle Paul said, "Therefore be careful how you walk, not as unwise men but as wise, making the most of your time, because the days are evil" (Ephesians 5:15–16). Two millennia since then, nothing has changed. Time is still a nonrenewable resource, and a big part of being wise is making the most of the time we're given. You have only a small window of time to give your words to your children, and once it closes there is no do-over. In chapter 2, we looked at the words you say. In this chapter, we looked at saying the words. The reality is you can't do one without the other.

One last word to add to this chapter is more by-product than goal, but its impact on your child's life will be lifechanging:

vocabulary. All of the different ways you engage in giving your words to your child will give them more than just verbal exercise. The growing storehouse of words in their mind will not be just so they can ace vocabulary tests. The impact of a broad and rich vocabulary has exponential effects on your child—the greater the vocabulary, the greater the impact. Consider just a few of the ways vocabulary works in your child's brain: it increases their listening and reading comprehension; it enables them to better understand contextual meanings; it increases their personal reading skills; it helps them to grasp complex concepts; it improves their communication skills; and most important in the context of this book, better vocabulary increases your child's ability to understand and express more complex theological and philosophical ideas. Madeleine L'Engle agrees: "We think because we have words, not the other way around. The more words we have, the better able we are to think conceptually."[12] Good vocabulary strengthens faith.

Our hope is that you will make the time to chart a path to a verbal home and that, because of what you do and the words that you say, your children, like those in Asaph's psalm, would "put their confidence in God and not forget the works of God, but keep His commandments" (Psalm 78:7). In the next section, we'll explore how to do that by combining both skills—the words you say and saying the words—for some specific kinds of verbal interactions with your children. The six word-giving exchanges—words that are personal, loving, nurturing, spiritual, wisdom, and believable—can help to put your feet on the path to a verbal home.

Parenting
VERBALOGISTICS

In his last letter, Paul told his protégé, Timothy, "Be diligent to present yourself approved to God as a workman who does not need to be ashamed, accurately handling the word of truth" (2 Timothy 2:15). That admonition can work for parents too, if giving your words is about handling accurately the word (and the words) of truth. But the first part is the key—make haste to be a faithful worker. The showing and telling skills for giving your words need to be learned and practiced, refreshed and rehearsed, if you want to be as effective as you can be in giving your words to your children. Take time together to assess the verbal atmosphere of your home—its current state, what you want to accomplish, and how to get there. Do you see a high percentage of RVEs (Reductionist Verbal Encounters) in your days? What is the impact of screen time on your children? How can you reclaim time in your family schedule to allow for more verbal time? What special times of interaction can you plan as a family? Keep a written or digital journal with ideas for stories you can share with your children. Start an illustrations log to record words, analogies, metaphors, and sayings that you can tell them. The more words you have on hand, the more you'll be able to demonstrate Proverbs 16:24: "Pleasant words are a honeycomb, sweet to the soul and healing to the bones."

Giving
WORDS

FOUR

Words That Are Personal

Let your speech always be with grace, as though sea-
soned with salt, so that you will know how you should
respond to each person.

Colossians 4:6

After Joel's first year of college at Seattle Pacific University studying communications, he knew he was not on the right path. He came home discouraged, and uncertain of what he should do next. Sally took him aside for a personal time with strong English tea, a freshly baked goodie, and soft piano music in the background to remove distractions and calm anxieties. She used their time together to draw him out, and when the time was right, she appealed to Joel's heart. "You are so talented, and you have a story to tell. If there were no restrictions, what would you want to do—right now—if you could do anything?" His unhesitating answer was completely unexpected and surprising. "I would go to Berklee

College of Music to learn more about music and being a professional musician."

Joel had always been musical—singing in the Texas Boys Choir, playing guitar and piano, writing songs, leading worship, attending the School of Worship in our large church—but before that moment he had never mentioned seriously studying music to us. Sally could see in his eyes that this was a legitimate and unspoken desire that had been burning in his heart, so she asked him what would keep him from going to Berklee. Joel shook his head and frowned in resignation. He said that the application deadline was only two weeks away, and he would need to go to Boston to audition for a spot. He explained that only a small percentage of applicants were accepted, and that he wasn't even sure if he was qualified to go to a serious music academy like Berklee. And he would need to write an original instrumental song for the audition. It all just felt like a bridge too far to him.

Sally looked him in the eyes and, also without hesitation, told him, "God has made you musical, Joel, and He will open the door if Berklee is where you need to be. They can say no, but what if they say yes? If this is right for you, right now, then you need to stop wondering about it, step out in faith, and give it your best shot." And with that personal encouragement bolstering his newfound resolve, Joel left their time together and started making plans. He completed the application, composed and practiced a new piece of instrumental piano music, and he and Sarah drove two thousand miles together to Boston, arriving in time for the last day of auditions. He was accepted and went on to be honored as composer of the year at his graduation three years later.

Since then, he has recorded numerous original instrumental piano albums, worked as an orchestrator in LA, composed and scored full-length movie soundtracks, written songs and performed with his sister in their Two Benedictions duet, and composed many sacred choral works for church worship. And it all started with a parent giving her words to a child in a personal time together.

A personal time with Mom or Dad (but especially Mom) in our family was somewhat like being given the VIP treatment. It was our way of letting a child know that they were, indeed, a very important person to us. It wasn't just a one-way event, though. When we felt that a child needed personal attention, we found that a hot drink and a cookie opened not just mouths, but hearts as well. That personal touch created a space and time for that child to open up about hopes, dreams, concerns, joys, and other heart matters. It was in those up-close-and-personal times that we could discern and respond to emotions, attitudes, and needs.

Jesus Gave Personal Words

You will not see the word *personal* very often in English translations of the Bible, but you will see the act of being personal throughout its pages, and especially in the life of Jesus. Books about discipleship often quote the "with Him" principle from Mark's Gospel: "And He appointed twelve, so that they would be with Him . . ." (3:14). It is a succinct two-word statement of how Jesus would be able in the span of just three years to make disciples who would change the world. They would be "with Him" as disciples following their rabbi, receiving and internalizing the words He would give to them, becoming like the Messiah who came to be Immanuel, "God with us." He would, of course, preach to multitudes and crowds, but His real ministry was always up close and personal, not only with His disciples but with all the people—loving them, having compassion for them, rejoicing with them, weeping with them, encouraging them, admonishing them, listening to them, and always giving them His words. He revealed to us a God who is engaged and personal.

Perhaps the most personal encounter by Jesus recorded in the Gospels is what is often called His "upper room discourse" and "high priestly prayer," the words, as He told His disciples, that were given to Him by God to give to them. Jesus and the Twelve had gathered for the Passover meal—the last time they would all be together before the events that would lead to His death on the cross. But before the meal began, Jesus did something that to the disciples must have seemed like an unthinkable act by their Master. As they entered the room with feet dirtied from a day on the Jerusalem roads, Jesus "poured water into the basin, and began to wash the disciples' feet and to wipe them with the towel with which He was girded" (John 13:5).

This was not what a respected rabbi and teacher should do—Jesus humbling and even humiliating himself to become a servant, washing His disciples' feet. But it was necessary for what was to come. After He had finished washing the last of the twenty-four dirt-caked feet, and had put His robe back on and reclined at the table, He explained why. The words He gave to them in that moment beautifully summarized His intent for the way He ministered, humbly and personally, and set an example that they, and we, should follow.

"Do you know what I have done to you? You call Me Teacher and Lord; and you are right, for so I am. If I then, the Lord and the Teacher, washed your feet, you also ought to wash one another's feet. *For I gave you an example that you also should do as I did to you.* Truly, truly, I say to you, a slave is not greater than his master, nor is one who is sent greater than the one who sent him. *If you know these things, you are blessed if you do them.*"

John 13:12–17, italics added

Jesus' actions and words in washing His disciples' feet set the tone for all that He was about to say to them that night in the upper room. Before they could hear those words and His prayer for them, Jesus let them know up front that if they wanted to be like Him, their "Teacher and Lord," it would start with being a servant.

The same is true for us today as we explore the idea of verbal parenting. Creating a verbal home begins with following Christ's example of personal ministry by first choosing to serve your children. The words you give in your personal interactions with them will be effective for Christ only if they come from the heart of a parent who is a servant like Christ—one who with humility of mind regards others, even their own children, as more important than themselves.

Even though there are no specific discourses or teachings by Jesus that can be reduced to a "How to Be a Verbally Personal Christian" lesson plan, just observing the example of Jesus in the Gospels can be enough. Whether the accounts of His personal and verbal interactions are with His closest disciples ("the Twelve"), with His many followers, or just with individuals in various settings, we can extract principles of what personal and verbal ministry looks like at home with our children.

He Responded Personally

A cursory study of the Gospels will find dozens of accounts of Jesus responding personally to people who come to Him. Many times, it is an adversary either challenging Him or asking legitimate questions. In either case, Jesus listened carefully and responded thoughtfully. For example, when a scribe asked Him, "What commandment is the foremost of all?" (Mark 12:28), Jesus personally and positively responded to the scribe. When Nicodemus came to Jesus at night to talk with Him and to ask legitimate theological questions, Jesus responded with thoughtful and serious answers to the Jewish leader's inquiries (see John 3).

If you want to emulate Jesus at home, you should always be ready to respond personally to your children's thoughts and questions. It will let them know that they are being heard by the most important person in their young lives, and it will give you the opportunity to use that moment of openness to give good words to your child. That's why no question, no matter how "childish," should ever be ignored or dismissed. A good parent will know how to respond positively to a childish question in a way that creates a personal connection to keep the door to their mind and heart open. To ignore a question—or worse, to give a negative response—says loudly to your child that they should not expect you to respond personally to them. Such a non-giving response will close their mind and heart to you. Give your child words that give life.

He Initiated Personally

Most of the stories about Jesus in the Gospels picture Him responding to people. However, He also initiated personal conversations with them. He broke cultural rules to ask the Samaritan woman at the well for a drink of water, and His words would change her life (John 4). After feeding the five thousand, He asked His disciples, "Who do people say that I am?" (Mark 8:27) to help them understand what was to come.

Initiating personally and verbally with your children at home can be either a planned exchange, or part of a teachable moment. In either case, you have words to give that you want your child to hear, but taking personal initiative in giving your words should be more than just a "now hear this" of verbal interaction; initiative is the essence of the intentional aspect of creating a verbal home atmosphere. Of course, we always had our verbal radar on so we could take advantage of teachable moments. But we also set aside time annually and monthly to talk about what we felt our children needed to hear from us, and how we could give them those words. To initiate simply means to begin something. To emulate Jesus, it means to intentionally begin verbal interactions, or personal encounters, with your children.

He Offered Direction

Much of what is recorded in the Gospels is in the form of Jesus' sermons, teaching, and prophetic messages. Those words could be given in either small and very personal settings (sitting in a boat by the shore of Lake Galilee, teaching in a home, walking along the road) or larger and less personal settings (Sermon on the Mount, feeding the five thousand, speaking to the crowds). Even in those larger settings, though, Jesus often was speaking personally to His disciples gathered around Him while the crowds listened in. Jesus was a teacher (a rabbi), and the nature of His instruction was direction—what it means to live a life that will please God. There were other more specialized kinds of messages, but according to John, "In Him was life, and the life was the Light of men" (1:4)—Jesus came to be a light to direct us out of the darkness. He had said the same thing during a feast in Jerusalem, when He contrasted the misleading messages of other teachers with His own message, saying, "I came that they may have life, and have it abundantly" (John 10:10). Jesus' lifegiving words of direction were always given personally and persuasively.

Emulating Jesus in giving words of personal direction might feel like a challenge for many Christian parents. You may be thinking, *I don't know enough of the Bible to give my child the kinds of words that Jesus would give.* But you don't have to be Jesus; you only need to be you. It all goes back to sharing personally from the well of the Spirit in your life. If you are walking with the Lord, reading His word, and finding direction for your own life from Him, then that is what you can share. Jesus said, "If you abide in Me, and My words abide in you, ask whatever you wish, and it will be done for you" (John 15:7). When you personally give the words that are in you to your child, you are directing them, just as Paul did with new and growing Christians: "Be imitators of me, just as I also am of Christ" (1 Corinthians 11:1). The best direction you can give is when you simply share with your children your own personal experience of what it means to live and walk with Jesus by faith.

He Affirmed and Encouraged

When Jesus looked out at the multitudes of people, "He felt compassion for them, because they were distressed and dispirited like sheep without a shepherd" (Matthew 9:36). That compassion and concern is expressed throughout the Gospel accounts when Jesus personally encouraged and affirmed people. When the disciples were troubled and feeling uncertain on the night of their last Passover in the upper room, Jesus personally encouraged them, "Peace I leave with you; My peace I give to you; not as the world gives do I give to you. Do not let your heart be troubled, nor let it be fearful" (John 14:27). He personally affirmed Peter's declaration of faith that He is the Messiah, saying, "Upon this rock I will build My church" (Matthew 16:18), and after His resurrection, He personally encouraged Peter (even after Peter's denial), telling him to "Tend My sheep" (John 21:17). There are many other admonitions and examples of encouragement in Scripture, but in the life of Jesus we see encouragement and affirmation expressed personally. Scripture tells us to be encouraging; Jesus shows us how.

Most parents will understand what it means to give their children affirming and encouraging words, since they themselves know what encouragement sounds like. But it's another thing to affirm and encourage personally. Affirming words are inherently personal because they address a child directly: "You're really good with your hands," or "I appreciated how you helped Mrs. Jones," or "You sounded very assured and skilled in your talk." Affirmation is not just flattery; it's personal acknowledgment of ability, accomplishment, character quality, or the like. Encouraging words require more thoughtfulness to make them personal: "I know you can do that because you have before," or "Pray about the decision and trust God to help," or "Just go for it and do your very best." Encouragement is not just a pep talk; it's instilling personal confidence looking forward on a task, opportunity, or choice. What makes either affirmation or encouragement personal, though, is that the words given are heartfelt—spoken from your heart to your child's heart.

He Asked Questions

Jesus liked to ask questions. It was an effective way to connect and interact personally with people. Who do you say that I am? Do you believe? Are you also going to leave? What does Scripture say? Do you love me? Whose likeness and inscription is this? Is it lawful to do good on the Sabbath? Which is easier to say, "Your sins are forgiven" or "Get up and walk"? What does it profit a man to gain the world but forfeit his soul? Questions can be powerful yet very personal tools of verbal interaction when they elicit a response and engage a conversation or dialogue. Jesus' questions were not random, but thoughtful, targeted, timely, and personal.

This word-giving skill is the easiest and most effective quality of Jesus' personal relational skills to emulate. With good questions, you're never at a loss for initiating a verbal interaction with your child, gently probing their heart and mind, and personally responding to whatever you learn from their answers. Questions can be general and impersonal ("What did you do today?"), or specific and very personal ("How did you feel when your friend said that about you?"), so start with general questions to ease your child into more specific ones. Just remember that your child's answer is not the end of the interaction, but the beginning. The purpose of good questions is to create an opportunity to speak into their heart and mind. There's no doubt about it—questions give you personal word-giving power.

He Told Parables and Stories

One thing about Jesus' personal interactions with others stands out—the stories. Jesus captured people's attention and imagination with His masterful use of the parable—simple stories of everyday life with deeper meanings and analogies. The fifty-five parables recorded in the Gospels make up about one-third of His words, which is perhaps also illustrative of the power of stories to stay in the memory so that the Gospel writers would recall them. Who can forget His stories about the good Samaritan or the sower or the prodigal son or the rich man and Lazarus? Whether He included a parable in His general teaching, or responded personally to those around Him with one, stories are a hallmark of the words that Jesus gave to others and to us. Long before books, radio, TV, and streaming videos became the media of storytelling, Jesus used His voice as a medium for His time, telling stories and parables that engaged His listeners' minds and hearts.

Personally connecting with your children through stories does not mean you need to tell complex parables like Jesus did. Like most parents, you will not have a store of such specialized stories, but you do have stories to share that will engage the imagination and hearts of your children—stories about your own life and experiences, stories from your childhood, stories you see in the news, or just stories you make up for the moment, especially telling simple parental parables that include your children as part of the story. For example, if your child is feeling fearful about an upcoming test, tell a story about a child (using their name) who overcomes their fear by climbing a mountain no one else has scaled. It can be a very simple story, but told personally and with added drama and expression, it can become not only a helpful image or analogy for your child, but a story they'll always remember.

In Book II of *Till We Have Faces*, C. S. Lewis's masterful retelling of the Greek myth of Cupid and Psyche, Orual recalls what her mentor, the Fox, once told her: "Child, to say the very thing you really mean, the whole of it, nothing more or less or other than what you really mean; that's the whole art and joy of words."[1] Those words are a glimpse into Lewis's own love and joy of words. In the same way, with just a little preparation and practice, stories can become for you a rich, meaningful, artful, enjoyable, and ultimately very memorable part of your personal verbal interaction with your children. When you tell a story with art and joy, you're adding mental glue to your personal words to make them stick.

Personal Means a Person and a Personality

Jesus is our best biblical example of giving words personally. He was, after all, "God with us," up close and personal, and His followers who were "with Him" recorded for us what that looked like. When we talk about emulating Jesus as a personal word-giver, though, those kinds of encounters are only half of the word-giving story. We learn from Jesus how personal word-giving achieves its *telos*—its desired end or purpose. In simpler terms, it's about how the message gets from giver to receiver. However, the other part of personal word-giving is about understanding what shapes and informs the words that you give. It is about understanding yourself as a person and a personality.

When Sarah was only a baby, some friends introduced us to the Myers-Briggs Type Indicator, or MBTI, as a way to understand our personality types. It was so helpful for us personally and in our marriage that we later incorporated our own expression of personality type in our first book, *Educating the WholeHearted Child*, to help parents understand how personality preferences influence both their own teaching styles and their children's learning styles. Word-giving, like teaching, is also shaped and influenced by your personality preferences—the "means" by which you give your words—so we cannot talk about word-giving without at least considering the role of personality.

The words we give to our children are never neutral, as though they are precisely measured and machined pieces we fit together and proudly present. Far from it. Your mind is more like a giant banquet hall, with tables filled to overflowing everywhere you turn with a mind-boggling array of foods and flavors, organized with signs wherever you look. In a blink of the mind's eye, you run up and down aisles of tables, choosing which foods, in what amounts, and with what seasonings to pile on your mental plate. And when you present your plate of mind food to your child—whether it is a little or a lot, neatly organized or a bit of a mess, carefully seasoned or not—you just hope that they will eat your words, enjoy them, and ask for more. That is the inside story of personality.

The analogy of a mind banquet of words brings to mind the prophet Jeremiah's words: "Your words were found and I ate them, and Your words became for me a joy and the delight of my heart; for I have been called by Your name, O LORD God of hosts" (15:16). As parents, we all hope our children will receive our words with the same joy that Jeremiah received God's words. But then, we know that God's words are perfect and unfailing, in contrast to our own words, which are served up by very imperfect (and sinful) persons with distinct (and sinful) personalities, to children who are just the same. Giving words can never be a neutral, calculated, well-ordered verbal interaction. Even at home with your children, your word exchanges will always be messy simply because messiness is a quality of being human. And even though we are sinful and broken as human creatures, which can make things even messier, we also have the image of our relational God stamped on our souls, and as believers, the Spirit of God working within us. Those divine marks ensure that we can relate to God and one another verbally through words.

Scripture has much to say about our personness and personality, but we cannot explore those ideas here. The best we can do is encourage you to do your own work for giving words personally. Here are three suggestions.

First, *know yourself.* Philosophers have carved up the Greek dyad "Know thyself" in multiple ways, but most people hear those two words and assume it simply means to understand yourself as a person—your beliefs, values, drives, desires, hopes, fears, loves, passions, pains, strengths, weaknesses, gifts, abilities, temptations, nonnegotiables. The goal of all that personal knowing is not necessarily to arrive somewhere, but to be on the path to becoming a self-confident and authentic person. You want to be a person who can be believed and trusted as a word-giver, because you're true to who you are.

Knowing yourself as a person is not always easy, though. It means being willing to be honest with yourself, and to personally own what you discover. It's not something that is best done alone. You can and should do much of that discovery with your spouse, even if it's just reading through a book together and talking about it. However, a neutral party can also help—a friend, mentor, counselor, pastor, spiritual director, personal coach. The more you're able to learn about yourself, the more you'll gain a sense of confidence and authenticity, and the more effective you'll become as a person in giving your words to your children.

Second, *accept yourself.* That can mean many things, but for the purposes of this book, *accepting yourself* means embracing who God has made you to be and what He has given you to do. It's about your identity in Christ, your story, your history, and your personality. It's also about accepting both the good and bad parts of your personal history and journey, and about finding where you fit into God's bigger story. The starting point of accepting yourself is God's complete and unconditional acceptance of you as a person. Accepting yourself is an act of trust in God's love.

We both found great freedom in being able to appreciate and accept our very different personality preferences. For us, it was the MBTI that provided language to talk about our personalities in a way that neutralized our differences as people. For you, it can be whatever personality model provides that same kind of language that enables you to talk about your differences positively. And the more you understand the personality dynamic as an adult, the more you'll see it at work in your relationship with your kids, and especially in your verbal interactions. Be yourself, with your personality, to become a more personal word-giver.

Finally, *be like Jesus*. As a Christian, there is more to your personhood than only who you are as a human being. You are also a spiritual being, a new creation in Christ, and "it is God who is at work in you, both to will and to work for His good pleasure" (Philippians 2:13). The Holy Spirit is God within you, always at work to make you more like Jesus because "it is no longer I who live, but Christ lives in me" (Galatians 2:20). You cooperate with that work because "the one who says he abides in Him ought himself to walk in the same manner as He walked" (1 John 2:6). To be a Christian is to become like Jesus.

Scripture makes clear that even though we can imitate Christ in our lives, becoming like Jesus is not just up to us, but up to God. That's why He sent His Holy Spirit. The writer of the book of Hebrews encourages us to "lay aside every encumbrance and the sin which so easily entangles us" and to "run with endurance the race that is set before us, *fixing our eyes on Jesus*, the author and perfecter of faith" (12:1–2, italics added). The simplest way to be like Jesus is to fix your eyes on Him and follow Him. When you do, the Holy Spirit will be at work in you. And when your children see you doing that every day, and hear you talking about it, you'll be giving your words to them in the most personal way possible.

— . —

Giving words that are personal to your children is about much more than just what to say and when. It is about being a real person with them—letting your words not only tell them what you think, but also reveal who you are. That is the only way your words will engage heart-to-heart with your children. If they sense you are on a path to becoming confident and authentic, not just in your spirituality but also in your humanity, they will naturally follow your lead. Then your words will be not only in their heads, but in their hearts; not just heard, but believed. That is what we all want of the words we give to our children.

We'll close with Paul's admonition to the Colossian believers about the words we give: "Let your speech always be with grace, as though seasoned with salt, so that you will know how you should respond to each person" (4:6). This is a picture of giving words that are personal. When you initiate a verbal interaction, you must know yourself and your listener to be able to offer grace to them, and you must know them personally in order to season your words in such a way that will be meaningful to them. The goal is not just to say something, but to give words that will elicit a response that will then allow you to respond. That's all about the dynamics of giving words that are personal. When you see that happening with your children, you are not just saying things, but you are giving them your words by personally engaging with their minds and hearts.

Parenting
VERBALOGISTICS

Find a nice bound blank book and title the first page "My Jesus Journal" (or "Our" if you'll keep it together as a couple, or use your first name). Start reading through the Gospels, noting in the journal whenever you find examples of how Jesus related personally to others when giving His words. Using one page for each example, at the top, write the date, the verse reference, a short summary title of the passage (for example, "Jesus and the Blind Man"), and a brief description of what Jesus does (one to two sentences). Then, under a "Be Like Jesus" header, describe generally what it would look like to emulate in your relationship with your children what Jesus does in the passage. Finally, below that paragraph, write the name of a child and make a specific plan for how to relate personally to them and what words you want to give. Do that for each child that you want to apply the passage to, or you can designate it for "All." Whenever you're able to follow through on that plan, put a heart and a date by that child's name. It will become a nice keepsake of ways you intentionally and purposefully related to your kids and gave them your words like Jesus.

FIVE

Words That Are Loving

Beyond all these things put on love, which is the perfect bond of unity.

Colossians 3:14

Joy's seventeenth-birthday breakfast was in May of 2012 in Colorado, in our warm and cozy nook between the kitchen and the den, a favorite spot for this family ritual. At that time of the day, the sunlight coming through the large bay window, with Clay's framed stained-glass lighthouse hanging in it, threw a welcome and colorful light across our honey oak table surrounded by six high-backed oak chairs. Before the birthday child (or parent) is allowed to come to breakfast, the table is deliciously prepared and staged. For Joy, ribbons and balloons hung from the light fixture above the table, over lighted candles and red glitter hearts. Around and in Joy's chair were a plethora of presents and cards from parents and siblings. Six Gmunden plates from our years in a

Vienna mission, used for special events like this, were filled and sitting on green chargers, and every inch of each place was taken up with the traditional birthday breakfast: Sally's homemade whole-wheat cinnamon rolls, her famous Polish eggs (a cheesy egg and hash browns concoction from her single years as a missionary in Poland), crisp bacon, fresh strawberries and blueberries, a glass of milk (for dunking, of course), and strong Yorkshire Gold English tea in a Gmunden cup. When all was ready, Joy was led into the room with her eyes covered, and at the big reveal we all joyfully sang "Happy Birthday."

As with a table full of Hobbits, for a table full of Clarksons the feast always comes first. We believe that food is good not just because it is tasty and satisfying, but also because it is good for the soul. The physical act of feasting prompts the brain to release endorphins—hormones that give the spirit a feel-good sensation that can release good words.[1] Following the feast, presents are opened, and then we settle into our birthday breakfast tradition—a time of spoken love and encouragement, looking back on the year just passed, given by each family member (no exceptions) to the birthday celebrant. For Joy, it had been an unusually full and transitional year as she prepared to leave home and start college that fall at Biola University in Southern California. She had completed several early college courses, worked with a local MOPS group and saved money, worked at our three Mom Heart Conferences, and was accepted at Biola with a scholarship. A local speech and debate club made an exception to allow her to join in the middle of their year, and she was able to compete in local and national tournaments, ending up placing eighth in the nation in speech and debate, and third in interpretation.

With teacups refreshed, we all settled into the heart of the birthday breakfast—verbally loving, affirming, and encouraging Joy. As each person spoke in turn for five to ten minutes, soul-affirming words of love and appreciation were spoken into her life. Of course, words of affirmation were shared about her accomplishments that year, and about her discipline and diligence to do so much so well. But even more, words were given about how, through it all, she was always engaging and helping other people, initiating and responding personally just like Jesus did. Specific personal examples of how she had spiritually encouraged a sibling, sacrificed her own needs to help another, or been a friend to those who needed a friend were recalled and relived. After everyone else had shared, Sally always had special words to share with the girls, so she ended the time with her loving thoughts and encouragements for her youngest child. Then, Joy was asked to share what she was hoping and dreaming for the year ahead and how we could pray for her. We then all prayed, this time speaking words of love for her and hope for the year ahead as she would leave home and venture into the world and the new life opening to her. Like every child who is honored at their birthday breakfast, Joy got up from the table full of words of love, given from hearts full of love for her.

Christian truth often gets expressed colloquially: "God won't give you more than you can handle," "Let go and let God," "When God closes a door He opens a window," or "Everything happens for a reason." But even biblically based aphorisms can become, using the term coined by Stephen Colbert, more "truthiness" than true. For example, "Love is a verb." It feels like it should be true, but when you look at the most common Greek word family for *love*, the verb *agapao* accounts for about 55 percent of that love, and the noun *agape* for about 45 percent. "Love is a verb" is true, but no more true than "Love is a noun." In the Clarkson home, we found that love is a verb only *after* it is a noun; that acts of love must be built on thoughts of love, which must be expressed with words of love. Perhaps love that is spoken makes it a verb, but still it was truer for us to say "Love is verbal." One way we lived out that truth was in our family birthday breakfasts.

Love Is a Gift Wrapped in People

The spiritual atmosphere in a home works the same way as the physical atmosphere of the earth—we can't live without it. The figurative air that a child breathes at home either fills their spiritual lungs with the lifegiving air of the Spirit (or breath) of God, or its absence leaves them deprived of the spiritual oxygen they need for life in the Spirit. This book is all about how to create a rich verbal atmosphere of the Spirit in your home, but how does that relate to the emotional atmosphere of love discussed in this chapter? We believe the two are intrinsically and inseparably linked. That is the meaning of our earlier suggested aphorism—love is verbal. We can have love in our hearts (love is a noun) and even do loving acts (love is a verb), but until love is put into words (love is verbal), it does not become spiritual oxygen that gives life to the one breathing it in.

It is the lifegiving words of love that tell us we are beloved by God and others, and that inform and form our own hearts for how we can obey God's two great commandments—to

114

love God and to love others. Remember what Jesus said: "It is the Spirit who gives life . . . the words that I have spoken to you are spirit and are life" (John 6:63). It is in His words that we find the life of the Spirit that gives us life. And since we bear the image of the God who is love, follow Christ who died for us because of love, and have love in us as a fruit of the Spirit, the verbal love we have to share comes from that spiritual life within us.

Birthday breakfasts gave us regular opportunities to contribute to the verbal atmosphere of love in our home. They were intentional and purposeful times set aside for expressing love for each member of the family. But they were also times to train our children how to verbally express love. Expressing words that are loving is an acquired skill learned mostly from observation and practice, both of which happened during our birthday breakfasts. Since we brought our own family experiences to our marriage, we had learning and unlearning to do as well. Sally had grown up in a verbally expressive and loving home, but it could also be judgmental. Clay, on the other hand, never heard or said the words "I love you" in his family until becoming a believer in his twenties. As we learned more about each other and what experiences we brought to our new family, we set out intentionally over the years to improve the experience for our own children.

However, we wanted them not only to learn loving words from traditions like our birthday breakfasts, but also to acquire the sensitivity to recognize and reject unloving words. We could prohibit certain "bad" words such as *stupid*, *hate*, and the like, but internal attitudes and emotions could still be expressed in negative verbal ways such as "You're mean," "I don't care," or "That's dumb." We realized we needed to sensitize and train our children's spirits to know, before they were ever verbalized, what causes words to be unloving and the harm those words can cause to a relationship. Paul was addressing the same issue when he admonished believers, "Do not let any unwholesome talk come out of your mouths" (Ephesians 4:29 NIV). Don't say unloving words; say loving words.

Love Has a Personality

But here's the catch: There is no one-size-fits-all prescription for how to train a child to do as Paul says. Any child can learn and understand what loving and unloving words sound like, but different personality types will require more or less training, will have varying levels of self-control, and will express loving words differently than others. You will have to learn how to appreciate those differences in your children, as well as understand how your own personality becomes a factor in your parenting. To help with that, we developed a model to make it easier for parents to understand their children's personality types. There are four types in our WholeHearted Personality model: **Doers** (the "I can do that!" child), **Helpers** (the "How can I help you?" child), **Movers** (the "Let's do it together" child), and **Shapers** (the "I have a better idea" child). Each child's type is further shaped by whether their mental focus is "active" (extroverted) or "reflective" (introverted), and whether they orient to life by "time" (predictability and structure) or "experience" (spontaneity and flexibility). There are many other good personality models, but the key is finding one that you can use to better understand how your children express love verbally to you, their siblings, and others. (You can download a free PDF of our WholeHearted Personality model from WholeHeart .org/pdf-downloads, Educating the WholeHearted Child, Teaching & Learning Styles. It's also available in chapter 8 of our book *Educating the WholeHearted Child*.)

Our family personality culture was like many others—a merry mix and menagerie of types, mental focuses, and life orientations. Our personality pot was constantly being stirred by those dynamics, so we were always learning more about how love is best expressed to one another, and always trying to follow Paul's advice, "Let all that you do be done in love" (1 Corinthians 16:14). We learned that loving *acts* tend to be more about emotional affirmation (that make one feel known and loved), and loving *words* are about verbal expression (that tell one how and why they are loved); both say that love is good, but only spoken loving words can create a heart-to-heart personal connection. Love is verbal, and there is no easy substitute for giving words of love. But verbal words of love can come in many forms, suited to a wide range of personalities for both giver and receiver.

As Sarah turned twenty-three in May of 2007, she was becoming the writer she always wanted to be, having written *Journeys of Faithfulness*, many short pieces and poems, and more recently a blog called *The Itinerant Idealist*. She was a thoughtful introvert and an unapologetic idealist who valued imagination, words, poetry, art, and beauty. Time at Oxbridge two years earlier had set her young heart on the University of Oxford, even though a master's degree in theology from her dream college was still years away.

Clay's personality is less wordy than others in the family, but no less thoughtful. He had happened upon a blank card with an image of a country girl who resembled Sarah, reaching across a wooden fence to pick a wildflower. "The Flower Picker," a 1900 Pre-Raphaelite painting by British artist John William Waterhouse, captured Clay's imagination for his first child. Soon he found himself writing a poem called "The Itinerant Idealist." He copied the poem into the card and recited it to Sarah on her birthday. One of the five stanzas reads "But in this march of madding moves | One girl against the tide | Against the lockstep of the crowd | She breaks their stilted stride | To follow music of her own | To find the seeds of others sown | The dreams of hearts revealed." Toward the end it says of the idealistic girl of the verse "Dull others, plodding, will not find | These seeds of beauty sown | But she, entranced by flowered fields | Will dream of seeds her own." Sarah delighted in her father's poem that lovingly said in verse, "You are special and loved, and I am wholly behind wherever your dreams may take you." Love is not always expressed in breakfast traditions or in teatime conversations; loving words can also be given quietly and creatively in a verbal story or poem.

Love Is a Language Learned

Of all the key truths of the New Testament, love stands out like a beautiful song running through its pages, but nowhere more melodiously than in the writings of Paul. Jesus said, "So in everything, do to others what you would have them do to you, for this sums up the Law and the Prophets" (Matthew 7:12 NIV). Paul reaffirmed those words in Romans, saying that the entire Law is summed up in a single command: "Love your neighbor as yourself" (13:9). In his poetic defense of unconditional love for the love-challenged Corinthian church, Paul elevates love, the "more excellent way" (1 Corinthians 12:31), over faith and hope, and in his words to the Colossian church he admonishes them to "put on love" (3:14) like a garment. He returns often to the truth that Jesus asserted at His Last Supper: "By this all men will know that you are My disciples, if you have love for one another" (John 13:35). Paul expends many words trying to capture the essence of that love, which is like a repeating melody in his symphony of truth for the church. If we want to find clues to what Paul thought loving words should sound like, two passages stand out.

First Corinthians 13 is inspired poetry, but behind that poetry it is essentially a practical checklist of what love is, what love is not, what love does, and what love will be. First, *what love is* (v. 4). Love is patient and kind. It is the "what you would have them do to you" part of Jesus' Golden Rule. Second, *what love is not* (vv. 4–6). Love is not jealous of others, so it does not brag, it is not arrogant, and it does not act inappropriately. And love is not self-seeking, so it is not provoked to anger; it does not hold a grudge, and it is not glad about wrong done to another. Third, *what love does* (vv. 6–8). Love rejoices in what is true, and to that end it bears, believes, hopes, and endures all things. Finally, *what love will be* (v. 8). Love is never failing—it will never fail or fall from its place as the "excellent way." Paul's words personify love, but they create a picture not of the words of love, but of the inward character, nature, and attitudes of love—the unconditional *agape* of God. Without that love, anything else seemingly good Paul might do—inspired speech, prophetic insight, personal sacrifices—amounts to nothing. And though it may sound idealistic, it is nonetheless a picture even for parents of the kind of love our children hope to find in us. Thank God that love is also a fruit of the Holy Spirit within us!

But what about words of love? This book is about giving your words, so what do words that are loving sound like? There are countless passages we could consider, but we'll focus on Paul's other inspired poem about love in Colossians 3:12–17, an extended analogy of love as pieces of clothing we as believers must choose to wear. We'll list below each piece of love's clothing that Paul mentions, and briefly explore how it can be verbalized in loving words to give to your children.

It's helpful to get some context first. Paul is reminding the believers in Colossae that they need to reject "anger, rage, malice, slander, and filthy language from your lips" and to "not lie to each other." The reason, Paul says, is because "you have *taken off* your old self with its practices and have *put on* the new self, which is being renewed in knowledge in the image of its Creator" (3:8–10 NIV, italics added). Don't miss the point of Paul's setup to what he is about to tell them about love—that putting on the new self should be demonstrated by a change in the words that come from their mouths. Therefore, Paul says, because they are God's people, they should "put on love" (v. 14). The word for "put on" means simply to put on clothing, but Paul uses the term only figuratively, thirteen times in six of his epistles. (Jesus also used it once.) Paul has words on his mind and heart as he expresses to the Colossians "As you are loved, put on love."

Put on a Heart of Compassion (v. 12)

Perhaps it is no coincidence that the first article of love we are to put on is a heart of compassion. The "heart" here is not *kardia*, the term Paul typically used. Rather, it and the term for compassion both refer to the bowels, or the gut. To Greeks, bowels represented the location of strong passions, but to Jews it was the place of tender affections, emotions, and mercy. Perhaps a "heart of affection" would be a more personal expression. When you are wearing a compassionate heart, the words you give your children will tell them how much you love them and care for them: "You are so special to us and we are so blessed," or "I just want you to know how much I love you today," or "We just love how God has made you such an amazing child."

Put on Kindness (v. 12)

This word is used exclusively by Paul in the New Testament—once about himself, seven times about God's kindness, and twice about God's people. There is also a sense of moral goodness in the Greek term, suggesting that this kindness is not just about being nice, but about goodness, character, and integrity. In the language of today, it is about authenticity. In giving loving words to your children, kindness might mean assuring them that your love for them is settled in your heart because of the Holy Spirit, and that your kindness for them is not a fickle thing: "You never, ever need to worry about our love for you," or "We love you because God loves you and we love God," or "Nothing you do can change my love for you."

Put on Humility (v. 12)

Paul wasn't writing to parents when he told the Philippians "With humility of mind regard one another as more important than yourselves" (2:3). Nonetheless, if we want to have the same humble attitude that Christ demonstrated, then we'll need to put on a humility hat every morning and wear it all day long. Most good parents will not be proud or selfish, and yet we all still need to ask how to make "humility of mind" a parental expression of love. Humility in its simplest expression is modesty or decency, so that may be easier to put into loving words: "We were wrong about that and we're sorry," or "This has been a difficult day and I apologize for being so grumpy," or "Would you forgive me for causing us to leave so late?"

Put on Gentleness (v. 12)

Jesus described himself as "gentle and humble in heart" (Matthew 11:29), so gentleness is another piece of love's clothing that we put on. Gentleness is often included in biblical lists of spiritual qualities of mature faith. It is also linked in the New Testament with the concept of discipline, which puts it on more solid parental ground. You may use the phrase "strict discipline," but the correct biblical phrase should be "gentle discipline" (see Clay's book *Heartfelt Discipline*). The words you give must be gentle to be loving: "You're a ball of energy today, so what can we do together?" or "It's wrong to hit your sister, so stay with me until you can apologize," or "You're a good boy, and I love you, but you need to stay in your room."

Put on Patience (v. 12)

Paul was a big fan of patience. As a fruit of the Holy Spirit, patience shows up in several other lists of character qualities of maturity, including "humility and gentleness, with patience, showing tolerance for one another in love" (Ephesians 4:2), with all four of those qualities also being mentioned in the Colossians passage. And if patience is a virtue, then parental patience gets bonus points. Every parent, no matter their children's ages, knows putting on patience is not an option, just as being ready to patiently speak loving words is not: "Tell me your joke again, because it's the best," or "I'll wait for you to get control and then we'll talk," or "You're really trying, I can tell, but let me explain it again."

Put on Forbearance (v. 13)

Paul links forbearance ("bearing with one another") and forgiveness ("forgiving each other") in this passage. The term he uses for forbearance, applied to interpersonal relationships with other believers, is used in that way only here and in the Ephesians 4:2 passage mentioned above. It is the idea of being a sustaining and upholding person. In other words, forbearance is the garment of love to put on that means you will stick with another person and endure for their benefit. It's more an assumed quality in parenting, but your children need to hear loving words of forbearance from you: "We are always here for you no matter what," or "I am with you in this all the way to the end," or "We will be faithful to God and pray for His blessing on our family."

Put on Forgiveness (v. 13)

Paul uses the verb *charizomai* here, which is derived from the noun *charis*, which means "a gift of grace." Underneath the idea of simply forgiving each other, or granting pardon, is the idea of a gracious gift or favor. But Paul's elaboration gives the full picture—it is for "whoever has a complaint against anyone," and is given freely "just as the Lord forgave you." In other words, forgiveness is an unconditional favor given to everyone in Christ's name. It is much more than a perfunctory "Sure, I can forgive you." It is a gift of love that even your children need to hear: "In our home, we always forgive one another in the Lord," or "Being mad at each other is not what the Lord wants, so let's forgive one another," or "Grace and forgiveness are how we defeat the grudge monster."

Put on Love (v. 14)

Finally, Paul says to "put on love." Not just a simple love, but *agape*—the unconditional love of God (John 3:16), the sacrificial love of Christ on our behalf (Ephesians 5:2), the first fruit of the Holy Spirit (Galatians 5:22), the core nature of God (1 John 4:8), the proof of being Christ's disciple (John 13:35), and the "greatest" Christian virtue (1 Corinthians 13:13). *Agape* is not just another random article of spiritual clothing to put on, but the final tunic that covers all the previous expressions of love: "And over all these virtues put on love, which binds them all together in perfect unity" (Colossians 3:14 NIV). *Agape* is used 117 times in the New Testament, a testimony to its central importance to the life of faith. Without it we are, in Paul's words, nothing. It would be futile to try to express this *agape* in loving words for your children here. Thankfully, though, the New Testament writers have already done that, so read those many scriptures with your children. Let them hear God's words of love, since they are, after all, God's words to you and your children.

The ABCs of Loving Words

The suggested words of love above can be a helpful starting place, but what about all the words of love not on the list? Is there a way to be ready to give words of love in any situation you'll confront in parenting? We always found it helpful to have a simple and memorable template or acrostic mentally tucked away to apply on the spur of the moment. For example, a favorite we used for home nurture is LifeGIFTS—asking during the day how we were giving our children gifts of Grace, Inspiration, Faith, Training, and Service. It didn't cover everything, but it helped to ensure that we would not miss good moments of parental discipleship. So, for giving loving words, let us suggest a similar template to help—the ABCs of Loving Words.

A: Words That Accept

The essence of *agape*, God's kind of love that Scripture calls us to emulate in our relationships with each other and the world, is unconditional acceptance—it is given freely, with no conditions or expectations of anything in return. In colloquial terms, it is love with no strings attached. The nature of God is perfect love within the Godhead—Father, Son, and Holy Spirit. Since your children bear the image of that relational God in their spirits, they are already hardwired to know and respond to that kind of love, so they are looking for it from you. Dr. Ross Campbell, in his book *Relational Parenting*, explains what loving a child that way means: "Unconditional love means loving a child no matter what. No matter what the child's abilities, assets, looks, or personality traits. No matter who the child may remind you of. No matter the history surrounding him. No matter what you expect of him."[2] So as you go through the day with your children, simply ask yourself, *Are the words I am giving to my children today loving words that tell them I accept them without exceptions or expectations?*

B: Words That Believe

Lady Bird Johnson was a groundbreaking first lady under her husband, LBJ, the thirty-sixth U.S. president. Although she was not a parenting expert, she advocated for children during her time in the White House. One expression of her simple wisdom has outlived her: "Encourage and support your kids because children are apt to live up to what you believe of them." Your children need to hear that you believe in them, in their potential and possibilities. We would regularly speak into our children's lives the possibilities of what they could do and how God might one day use them. We wanted to create word pictures in their minds of ideals to live up to, and of who they could become. Even more, though, your children need to know that you believe the best about them. They need to know, despite their immaturity, that you believe in their inherent goodness as God's creation, and in their inherent ability to value the goodness of the God who made them. You are helping to prepare in them an "honest and good heart" that will be receptive to God's word and to your words. So as you go through the day with your children, simply ask yourself, *Are the words I am giving to my children today loving words that tell them I believe in them, without holding back or hesitation?*

C: Words That Commit

Commitment is the glue that will hold all the words of love together in your children's hearts. Dr. Tim Kimmel, director of Family Matters ministry, says this about commitment: "Love is the commitment of my will to your needs and best interests, regardless of the cost. . . . Love is about making decisions based on the covenant we have with that person."[3] Your commitment to your children is roughly analogous to God's faithfulness—you know that God will be faithful to His promises, and that gives you confidence to follow Him. But we knew that our commitment to our children was about more than just emotional or even spiritual security—it was also about our commitment to the personal God we talked about, to each another as marriage partners, and to the biblical truths that defined and directed our lives. Our children needed to hear that our commitment to what we believed was true and trustworthy, and even more that it was consistent and uncompromised. So as you go through the day with your children, simply ask yourself, *Are the words I am giving to my children today loving words that tell them I am committed to them without reluctance or reservation?*

— • —

Your children will hear many modern maxims about love, but most will be just bits and bites of truthiness from pop culture. When it comes to the words you give to your children, as important as love is, it is not the only thing they need. And yet love, arguably, must be the first word among all the other words you will give them, just as Paul suggested to the Colossians: "Beyond all these things put on love, which is the perfect bond of unity" (3:14).

God's love is a unifying and bonding virtue, one that will hold together all the words you will give to your children, just as the "God [who] is love" (see 1 John 4:8) holds together all His creation. Scripture would be meaningless without the beginning-to-end thread of God's faithful love, and our parenting will be passionless and powerless without it. Without His love leading the way, we would all lose our way as Christian parents. As you consider the words you are giving to your children, love may not be all you need, but love is what you need above all.

Parenting
VERBALOGISTICS

One good acrostic deserves another, especially one for "LOVE" in a chapter about love. This is a simple devotional outline you can use alone or with your spouse to discover and plan ways to verbalize loving words for your children.

WORDS OF LOVE: First, pick a topic related to love that you want to study. An example would be any of the apostle Paul's words of love listed in his poetic expressions of divine love in 1 Corinthians 13 and Colossians 3:12–14.

MY LOVE AT HOME: Next, use the LOVE acrostic below to study the topic you've chosen. Write down what you discover in a journal or notebook.

128

L—LOOK at yourself: Examine your experience with the subject of love you choose, both as a receiver and a giver. Write a profile of what you see.

O—OPEN your Bible: Do a concordance or topical Bible study of the subject. Write down the verses or passages that you feel are most important.

V—VOICE your heart: Write out several sentences you can use to verbalize those love words to your children—not just general sentiments, but the words you would say.

E—ENJOY your child: Plan a time when you can naturally give your words of love to your children. Make it a positive and fun family time.

GOD'S LOVE IN ME: Choose a scripture memory verse for yourself. Put it where you will see it every day, whether in print or digitally online or in an app.

SIX

Words That Are Nurturing

*Fathers, do not exasperate your children; instead, bring
them up in the training and instruction of the Lord.*

Ephesians 6:4 NIV

In 1999, we moved from Texas to Colorado, to the Front
Range of the Rocky Mountains, in Monument, a bedroom
community twenty miles north of downtown Colorado
Springs on Interstate 25. Two miles west of the interstate
and Monument Hill, sitting at about the same 7,000-foot
altitude, our foothills home was wedged into a man-made
hillside cleft with only sprawling acres of national forest
for a backyard. Clay and the boys would spend many hours
walking and talking along the trails of Mount Raspberry and
Mount Herman, but they also enjoyed a "Boys' Night In"
together at home, taking journeys along more spiritual paths.

The first year in Monument, when Joel was about thirteen
and Nathan about eleven, Clay would meet with them every

Wednesday night to read aloud and discuss Robert Lewis's popular book about guiding sons into manhood, *Raising a Modern-Day Knight*. It was a strategic and intentional time for nurturing with lifegiving words of grace. They would gather in Clay's comfortable and manly home office, close the door, and enjoy hot chocolate and a homemade treat designed to prime the discussion pump. They started the time just talking about guy things, to open heart doors, and then they would read and discuss a chapter of the book. Lewis talks about the ideals, ceremonies, community, and legacy of knighthood, so their discussions found many interesting life trails to explore. Clay purposely used the time to share words of dadly wisdom and lifegiving nurture that would give the boys grace for their lives as they turned the corner from childhood into young manhood.

Clay and the boys also had their Boys' Night Out when they would go out to eat, usually at a local fast Italian restaurant with pizza, lots of breadsticks, and the coveted self-serve soft drink machine. It was a time to just eat and talk—feeding their growing-boy appetites and their developing spirits. For them, it was grace that tasted good.

These times together culminated in a special ceremony and blessing Clay had for each boy as he turned thirteen. There was the traditional birthday breakfast, of course, but the afternoon teatime was a ceremony to launch our boy into young manhood. It included scripture readings, personal charges about honor and purity, and prayer, but most of all, it included . . . the sword. Each boy received a beautiful Knights Templar sword, crafted of fine polished metals in silver and gold plate from Toledo, Spain. It would become a cherished keepsake and reminder of their charge to be a noble knight for God—a man of biblical conviction, integrity, bravery, and honor. Along with the sword, they also received a silver cross pendant or a silver ring, a simple token to remind them of their commitment to Christ. All the nurturing words given at these special times were words of grace that brought life.

Grace and Nurture

This chapter is about words of grace and nurture. Since the word *grace* pops up dozens of times in modern English translations of the New Testament, while the word *nurture* is literally nowhere to be found, you might wonder why we have them together. Properly understood, *nurture* is the act of cultivating life—protecting, preserving, and nourishing a living thing. *Grace*, then, is how God gives us His life (it is an unmerited gift), and *nurture* is how we can give God's grace of life to one another. It's not the only way we give grace, but nurture is a spiritually lifegiving act. And we'll go one step further to say that for children, biblical nurture is God's grace given in words.

That is nowhere more clearly seen than when Paul instructs parents in Ephesians 6:4 to "bring [your children] up in the training and instruction of the Lord" (NIV). However, here's a paraphrase that better expresses Paul's admonition: "Parents, stop frustrating your children. Rather, nurture them with the words of instruction and guidance that come from the Lord." He uses the term *ektrepho*, a compound Greek word that taken literally means "to feed from." Parents were to nurture their children by feeding them with words of "training and instruction." And those words were to be "of the Lord," or coming from the life of God, who is now alive in their hearts as parents. Paul's words reflect the words of the Shema that they would recite every day: "These words . . . shall be on your heart" (Deuteronomy 6:6). The life of God is in the words, and children receive those words from nurturing parents.

In the Ephesians passage, Paul sets the standard for what Christian parents should do to nurture their children. But in 1 Thessalonians, he creates a word portrait of how that kind of nurturing parent should actually behave. Though he describes his own behavior toward the church using the language of parenting, his words are the clearest picture in the New Testament of Paul's personal conviction of what a Christian mother and father should be like. He reminds them that he was "gentle among you, as a nursing mother tenderly cares for her own children" (2:7). Then he describes his commitment to them, "as a father deals with his own children, encouraging, comforting and urging you to live lives worthy of God" (2:11–12 NIV). And the reason he says he behaved that way is the very heart of giving grace with nurturing words: "We loved you so much that we were delighted to share with you not only the gospel of God but our lives as well" (2:8 NIV).

Nurture is God's grace put into words. Paul clearly makes that connection between words and grace when he instructs the Ephesians to stop using destructive words, and to use only words that build others up according to their needs and "give grace to those who hear" (4:29). We should not use our words to tear others down, but to build others up in the Lord, so we can give words of grace to them. That's what words are for—to give grace to others. Tim Kimmel reminds us, "Grace-based parents spend their time entrusting themselves to Christ. They live to know God more. Their children are the daily recipients of the grace these parents are enjoying from the Lord."[1] And that grace will be given in words.

The highest purpose of the words we give to our children is that words are a means of grace—they create messages of love, acceptance, and forgiveness that give grace to others. C. S. Lewis, in his essay "Meditation in a Toolshed," recounts observing a sunbeam shining into a dark shed through a crack above the door. Looking *at* the beam, he sees only the beam itself. Looking *along* the beam, he sees the sun and objects within the beam's path. Lewis says, "We must . . . deny from the outset the idea that looking *at* is, by its own nature, intrinsically truer than looking *along*. One must look both *along* and *at* everything."[2] We can look *at* the beam of grace as a concept to define and explain it theologically and intellectually—what Scripture says it is and does. However, it isn't until we look *along* that beam of grace that we can see what it really is—that God is its source and power, words are its means and form, and it gives life to those along its path. When we give words of grace to our children, we are looking along that path not only to see how grace gives life, but to be part of the life that it gives.

Giving Blessings to Your Children

Words that are nurturing can also be called a blessing given to your children. Scripture is full of blessings, and though we are not able here to survey all those accounts, we cannot talk about nurturing words of grace without talking about blessing our children. The most common word in the Old Testament for that kind of blessing is *barak*, which literally means "to kneel down" or "to praise." It is a word picture of giving honor to the one who is being blessed. The most common word for *blessing* in the New Testament is *eulogia*, a compound word in Greek that literally means "good word." However, it is no coincidence that the Greek word for grace, *charis*, can also be translated as "blessing."

There are many accounts in the Old Testament of God blessing His people—the first, of course, being when God blessed Adam and Eve with the command to be fruitful and multiply. Other familiar passages include God's blessing for Aaron and his sons, for the Babylonian exiles, and for Israel before entering the Promised Land. But there are also family blessings, when a father blesses his children, which are the blessings we want to learn from and encourage. There is the familiar story of fraternal twins Jacob and Esau, the only sons of Isaac and Rebekah, when Jacob tricked their father into giving the blessing of the firstborn to him rather than Esau. Even though it is mostly a good example of a bad example, we still are able to hear the positive parental language of a Jewish father's blessing in it (see Genesis 27:27–29). A similar passage is Israel's (Jacob's) blessing on his twelve sons before his death in Egypt. Jews today still bless their children on Shabbat (Sabbath), but now, along with traditional blessings, families have a great deal of freedom in choosing what to include in the blessing. They may give their own words of blessing.

In the New Testament, we have the example of Jesus when He "took the children in his arms, placed his hands on them and blessed them" (Mark 10:16 NIV). We also know that blessing in the New Testament is primarily focused on God, the One "who has blessed us in the heavenly realms with every spiritual blessing in Christ" (Ephesians 1:3 NIV). Though there is no form or formula for a family blessing, there are certainly passages of Scripture that can be transformed into blessings for children. In a formal Christian family blessing, a parent cannot go wrong by simply speaking words of Scripture that will bring their child into all the blessings of Christ.

It's never too late to create a formal family blessing for your children, but if they are still young, you should plan how to make that practice a part of your family traditions. Giving a blessing, though, must always be more than just a one-time ritual or event—it should happen every day in the nurturing words of grace that you give to your children. Whenever you verbally nurture them, you are blessing them.

Gary Smalley and John Trent, in their book *The Blessing*, say it straight out: "We should not be surprised, then, that the family blessing hinges on being a spoken message. . . . In the Scriptures, a blessing is not a blessing unless it is spoken."[3] Bringing the various scripture pieces together, if you want to establish the tradition of giving a Christian family blessing to your children, consider including several elements in the nurturing words that you give:

- First, there should be **Affirmation.** Lay your hands on your child and say their name. "Mary Elizabeth Jones, our beloved daughter, we bless you today in the name of our Lord, Jesus Christ." This is the physical connection, but even more it is spiritual, because saying their name makes it personal by affirming who they are in your family. Continue the affirmation with "You have" words, looking back to the past to affirm your child's presence and value in your family. ("You have been our treasure.")

- Then, there should be **Confirmation** ("You are" words). In these words, you are giving language to your child that will answer for them the fundamental questions every human being asks: Who am I? Why am I here? Where am I going? These are positive and affirming "you are" words that only you will know how to say because you know your child. The words should tell your child of their great present value and worth in your eyes and God's, and of their acceptance by you and God. ("You are a lover of people and a giver of grace. You are loved greatly by us as a gift of grace to our family.")

- Finally, there should be **Expectation** ("You will" words). In these closing words, you are verbalizing what you expect God will do in their life—their purpose, unique gifts, place in His kingdom, eternal destiny as a recipient of Christ's blessings as His child, and more. ("You will be blessed of God with His peace and presence.") Here you will also formally offer "we bless" words to express your own parental commitment to your child's future success in life and fruitfulness as a child of God.

The ACE acrostic above that we suggested is based on Paul's opening blessing in his letter to the church in Philippi (see Philippians 1:1–9), a body of believers he deeply loved. We suggest it only as a form you can adapt, not as a formula. In the end, your family blessing will be your own, formed by the words of grace and nurturing that God gives to you to give to your children. You should take time to craft your words carefully, and then record them meaningfully for your children, whether in an audio or video recording, in a digital form such as a web page, in printed form, or all of those. Your family blessing will be nurturing and lifegiving words that you give to your children for the rest of their lives, so memorialize them in a way that your kids will be able to take them beyond your home.

The Grace of a Christian Home

Planning for special Christian family blessings for your children helps ensure that you give them specific words of grace from your heart that will nurture God's life in them. However, though a family blessing is a beautiful tradition to add, it should be just a starting place. Too many Christian families wrongly believe that their Christian home automatically provides the family blessing for their children. Too often, the idea of that Christian home is defined by what the children are doing—Sunday school, Bible club, Christian friends and activities, Christian books, music and videos, and more. Those may all be good things, but they do not make a home "Christian." If parents are not actively nurturing their children with the life of Christ, then it is a misnomer to call their home Christian. Only you can make your home a Christian home.

God commanded the parents of Israel in the Shema to continually teach their children, all the time and in every place. In the same way, Paul commanded Christian parents to nurture their children continually in the "training and instruction of the Lord" (Ephesians 6:4). That is how you give them words to have the grace they need for life. A family blessing is one means of grace, but there are other ways to give nurturing words of grace that should be part of your daily life. Here are three commonly accepted means of grace applied to the home for giving words to your children:

- **Scripture**—Reading the Bible aloud is giving God's words verbally. The book of Hebrews says that "the word of God is living and active and sharper than any two-edged sword" (4:12). It is not just words on a page, but it is alive with the Spirit of God, and it can pierce hearts with its truth. It is "the sword of the Spirit, which is the word of God" (Ephesians 6:17). Read full passages and chapters so your children hear the full context and the flow of thoughts and truths. Scripture is grace in print.

- **Prayer**—Praying aloud with your children is inviting them into your conversation with the living God, who is present with you in your home. Keep prayer "living and active" by praying the words of Scripture as a family, changing pronouns to personalize the reading. Psalms are particularly good for family prayers and praises. Your words are being given to God, but they are also being heard and received by your children so they are nurturing and lifegiving. Prayer is grace in words.

- **Fellowship**—This means of grace is often seen in the context of church, but it is also bringing other like-minded believing families into your home. Your children need to receive grace not just from you, but from others who share your beliefs and life in Christ. This *koinoia*, or partnership, is a communal sharing in the life of God—bearing one another's burdens, encouraging one another, and stimulating one another to love and good deeds. Fellowship is grace in person.

Gifts of Grace in Lifegiving Words

We've suggested several specific *means* of grace for giving nurturing words to your children, but we also want to suggest several specific *messages* of grace—some actual words to give to your children that will be nurturing and lifegiving for them. Earlier, in chapter 2, we said that *charis*, the Greek word for grace, means a gift from God that brings joy, mercy, or favor. In that sense, as we said above, grace is also a blessing. For grace to be a gift or a blessing for your children, though, it needs to be given in words. Whatever the means of grace may be, it should always carry a message of grace. We think of these messages as "gifts of grace." Most parents know how to give words of love—"I love you," "I'm so glad you're my child," "You're very special to me." Similarly, they know instinctually how to give words of encouragement— "You can do it," "You look great today," "That was amazing." However, saying words that are "gifts of grace"—giving words that are meant to help form your child's self-worth and self-confidence—might not always feel as natural. The messages we suggest below are just a few examples of the kinds of ways you can give "gifts of grace" to your children.

The gift of "You are secure"

Depending on their age, life can be either mysterious or confusing for your children. No matter how much you try to create a secure home, they hear stories of broken homes from friends, or they have thoughts that they think you would find unacceptable. In the midst of difficult and uncertain times, they can also harbor fears they might not share freely, but they are still looking to you for security and stability. Your grace-giving words can reassure them: "You can share anything that's in your heart and I will not be surprised. I was a child once, and I remember what it was like. I am here for you." "Life is kind of scary right now, but I want you to know that you are safe and secure in our home. We will take care of you." "I know you have many thoughts and concerns, but you can be sure that God is with you and will never leave you. He has always been faithful to us."

The gift of "You are worthy"

There are some thoughts a child may not have on their own, but when you express those thoughts for them, it helps to instill a positive self-awareness that will be a helpful part of their personal formation. Your younger child will not think about whether they are a burden on you, but they still need to hear that they are not, while an older child with more knowledge about finances, family choices, and such might be more aware of those matters and need more reassurance. Your gift of grace can free your child from carrying the burden, consciously or not, of being a burden. "Have I told you recently what a blessing you are to us? You were a gift to us from God." "God, our Father in heaven, is our Provider. We trust Him to care about us just as your father cares about you." "We thank God that you are our child. The way He made you is just what we wanted. We can't imagine our family without you."

141

The gift of "You are special"

Children become aware at a young age of all the factors that make them different from other children—personality, appearance, capabilities, ethnicity, handicaps, and more. Whether you hear about it or not, all children are caught up in the comparison game, and it only gets more intense the older they become. The dangers of playing that game can be overconfidence in factors they perceive as good, or insecurity from factors they perceive as bad. Media and social media only make the comparison game unwinnable. Your words of grace can help your children reject the game and develop a healthy self-concept of their identity in Christ. "We're all different, but we're all the same. Everyone wants to be accepted just as God has made them. That's the person we know and love." "The things that make you different also make you special. No one else is like you. We love you just as you are." "You are fearfully and wonderfully made by God. Your personality is just what God intended. He has a purpose for how He made you."

The gift of "You are capable"

Intellectual and physical abilities become another—and more insidious—area of comparison: Who is smarter and who is stronger? In school, those can become a social sorting mechanism beyond a child's control, with grades creating an intellectual caste system and sports a meritocracy of physical abilities. When a child does not excel in one or the other, they can feel socially handicapped regardless of other abilities and positive qualities. If your child attends a school, your words can help them navigate those waters with grace and build self-confidence in their own abilities and capabilities.

Your words of grace can become anchors in their hearts of affirmation and acceptance. "You sing so well. Would you like to try singing in the children's choir? I think you would enjoy it." "Some children are good with numbers, others with words. Let's find out together what you're best at." "What makes you happy when you're doing it? That will be our clue to explore how you can use those abilities."

The gift of "You are lovable"

Every child needs to be loved, but they also need to feel lovable. It's one thing to tell your child you love them, but they may also need to know that they are lovable to others. A child can appear to be confident and engaged but struggle privately with a low sense of self-worth and feelings of not being acceptable, or even of rejection. There can be a variety of factors feeding a quiet and often hidden self-doubt—personality, limitations, body issues, experiences—but words of grace from a loving parent can help create a better self-dialogue. "It's harder growing up now. Why don't we meet each week to see what God says about His love and care for you? Just you and me." "Making new friends can be hard. Just be the kind of person you would want to know—friendly, kind, interested, and loyal—and a friend will come." "You are lovable and acceptable just as you are. You never need to try to be someone that you're not. You are the best version of you that there is."

— • —

To close this chapter, we need to go back to the beginning. We've been talking about nurture and grace, and how those are relational channels of lifegiving for your children.

To put uncomplicated handles on those words, grace is how God gives His light and life to us, and nurture is how we give God's grace to our children and others. Most important, though, grace and nurture are given by words. But there's one more thing we need to say: Nurture that gives grace must be Christocentric. In other words, biblical nurture is not a neutral and detached engagement with your children. It's not just about giving them a comfortable life so they feel loved and content. Biblical nurture is about the grace that is realized and centered in Christ. The apostle John, in the preamble to his Gospel, said that Jesus, "the Word [Who] became flesh," was the full embodiment of God's abundant and inexhaustible grace: "For of His fullness we have all received, and grace upon grace" (1:14, 16). To see God's grace, we must look to Jesus.

But as unfathomable as the incarnation of God in the person of Jesus Christ can seem to our finite minds, John suggests there is even more to it. He says, "For the Law was given through Moses; grace and truth *were realized* through Jesus Christ" (1:17, italics added). He asserts that grace and truth literally came into being through Jesus. In some way we cannot fully comprehend, the grace and truth of God were incarnated in the person of Jesus. So if nurturing your children is about giving them words of grace and truth, then your nurture must be from, for, and about Jesus. As John also said about the Word, "In Him was life, and the life was the Light of men" (1:4). And Jesus said, "I am the Light of the world; he who follows Me will not walk in the darkness, but will have the Light of life" (8:12). Biblical nurture is giving your children words of grace that give them the light and life of God.

Parenting
VERBALOGISTICS

Nurture is about giving the light and life of God's grace to your children. It can be likened to growing a garden—you water your children with your words and God's word, and you give them the light of God's presence so they'll grow with God's life. But as with a garden, you need a thoughtful plan to be sure your nurture produces life. As we mentioned in chapter 5, early in our parenting, we developed an acrostic to help make sure we were nurturing our children. It's called LifeGIFTS, and it's just a simple lens to evaluate how we were doing at giving our children gifts of life. We would use the acrostic to plan ahead for giving each gift by Training (actions and attitudes), Instruction (understanding, wisdom, faith), and Modeling (examples to imitate). For the purposes of *Giving Your Words*, you can use each of the gifts to plan the nurturing words about your children that you want to give to them. Here are the five GIFTS:

> G—Grace: The gift of grace is the desire and ability to relate personally and purposefully to God and people.
> I—Inspiration: The gift of inspiration is the desire and ability to view all of life in the light of God's sovereignty and purpose.
> F—Faith: The gift of faith is the desire and ability to study God's word and apply its truths to every area of life.
> T—Training: The gift of training is the desire and ability to grow in Christian maturity in the power of the Holy Spirit.

S—Service: The gift of service is the desire and ability to minister God's grace and truth to the needs of others.

The LifeGIFTS model for Home Nurture is fully developed and explained in our book *Educating the WholeHearted Child* and in Sally's book *The Ministry of Motherhood.*

SEVEN

Words That Are Spiritual

You also, as living stones, are being built up as a spiritual house for a holy priesthood, to offer up spiritual sacrifices acceptable to God through Jesus Christ.

1 Peter 2:5

Scrapbooking was not in the Clarkson gene pool, so we rarely captured family moments beyond random photos and occasional mementos. But 2008 was different. The twenty-eighth anniversary of our annual family day was epic. It was the kind of stunning August day that, after a two-year detour in humid Tennessee, made us glad we'd moved back to Colorado in 2006—blue skies, bright sun, cumulus clouds, light breezes, mid-seventies. We were in Mueller State Park, a Rocky Mountains garden of trees, rocks, and trails, nestled at eight thousand feet, just below the western slope of the famous fourteener Pikes Peak, which we see every day from our home in Monument. Our children were all growing up—Sarah was twenty-four, Joel twenty-one, Nathan nineteen, and Joy thirteen—but there was an energy and *joie de vivre* infecting the whole tribe that made it a day for the family ages.

Since our first outing there in 1999, it had become the favorite destination for our family day celebrations—always the same picnic lunch of homemade goodies (fried chicken fingers, baked beans, chocolate sheet cake), followed by long hikes, debates and discussions, and family photos. Unlike later years when six iPhones would create Dropbox folders full of photos, that year we were armed only with a low-tech, faux SLR digital camera. Nonetheless, we took several hundred photos of surprisingly good resolution that Clay, in a fit of secretive fatherly focus, creatively compiled and narrated in a one-hundred-page photo album to tell the story of that afternoon in the mountains—portraits, group shots of all kinds, frolicking down hills, fun boy fisticuffs, kids on fallen trees, kids on rocks, limb-throwing contests, and more. It became a rarely captured Clarkson family moment.

If a picture is worth a thousand words, then that photo album is valued at 134,000 words, which is probably a good estimate of family day words shared over the years before and including that day. Of all our Clarkson traditions, family day is undoubtedly the oldest and best at exemplifying our commitment to giving our words. In our "Mueller time" in the mountains, words are given casually; but in our home time in the morning, before the forty-minute drive to Mueller, words are given intentionally. Family day mornings always start with Sally's homemade cinnamon rolls to warm up spirits, then moving to the den with cups of preferred hot beverages, and then it's all about words. The rest of the morning is focused on sharing memorial stones, based on the story in the book of Joshua. When God held back the Jordan River so the Israelites could cross the riverbed on dry ground into the promised land of Canaan, Joshua removed twelve stones from the middle of the Jordan and set up an altar at Gilgal just outside Jericho. He told the Israelite parents gathered there that when their children asked about the stones, they were to tell them what God had done that day (see Joshua 4). The stones were there to remind their children, and them, of God's faithfulness and power. Our memorial stones are much less weighty, being drawn and written on paper, but no less meaningful.

The primary purpose of our annual family day is remembrance—we decided early in our marriage that we wanted to set aside a sacred time every year, typically on a weekend near our anniversary, to remember and record specific ways that God has been faithful to us as a family in the year before. When the kids were younger, we would make a list of ways that God had been faithful, write each one on a special sheet of paper, and pass them out to everyone to draw pictures to represent God's faithfulness to us. We still have all those memorial stone drawings, but as the kids grew older and discussions grew longer, we focused on simply remembering and writing down God's acts of faithfulness. The 2008 rememberings were full of changes and challenges as we had seen God provide for needs, open doors of new opportunity, bless us in unusual ways, expand our ministry after a difficult season of loss, affirm our children's talents and skills, create new friendships and relationships, and more. We recalled and praised God for thirty such memories, a family day record high, all recorded on paper for posterity.

Later that night, over dinner on the deck, we took time to thank and praise God for all of them, and then to share what we all wanted to pray for the year ahead, writing down those prayer requests as well. It was an epic family day—words were given from all sides that will always be remembered.

Saying Spiritual Words

More than all the feasting and fun, though, there is one overused and much maligned—though very biblical—word that defines our family day: *spiritual*. Our family day words are intentionally, purposefully, and unreservedly spiritual. The day would make absolutely no sense apart from all our words about spiritual truth, spirituality, the spirit world, and the Holy Spirit. We gave our children spiritual words because that's what God's word says—we are spiritual creatures with an immaterial soul in our material bodies (1 Thessalonians 5:23); we are loved by a divine Creator who is spirit (John 4:24); we have been transformed in our own spirits by the Spirit of God (2 Corinthians 5:17); we have a new mind in Christ by the Spirit (1 Corinthians 2:16); we are engaged in a spiritual battle with spiritual powers in a spiritual world that we cannot see (Ephesians 6:12); we will live after death as resurrected spiritual beings with glorified bodies (1 Corinthians 15:42–44); we no longer live by the sinful flesh but by the Spirit (Romans 6:4–7; 8:5–8); and there's more, but you get the picture. If you feel we're somehow over-spiritualizing our Christian life, then you have not read your Bible very carefully.

When we stepped by faith into the promises of the gospel, we entered the realm of the spiritual—a new place that meant learning a new language for understanding it and for communicating its realities to others. As parents, we give words to our children that are spiritual because we are all on a spiritual journey together as a family learning how to live in the Spirt. God has designed us to talk about, share, experience, and teach what that spiritual journey is all about verbally. Why? Because God has spoken. He is a God of words, giving His words in human languages, in His word the Bible, and in the Word (*Logos*), Jesus: "And the Word became flesh, and dwelt among us, and we saw His glory, glory as of the only begotten from the Father, full of grace and truth" (John 1:14). The incarnation, when God became man in Jesus, showed us the bridge between the natural life and the spiritual life. We know it is true because Jesus died and was resurrected to that life, and we know because of our faith in Him that we will also be resurrected and "shall not perish, but have eternal life" (John 3:16). Paul says that spiritual life, in all its dimensions, is a verbal life:

> For who among men knows the thoughts of a man except the spirit of the man which is in him? Even so the thoughts of God no one knows except the Spirit of God. Now we have received, not the spirit of the world, but the Spirit who is from God, so that we may know the things freely given to us by God, *which things we also speak*, not in *words taught by human wisdom*, but in those *taught by the Spirit*, combining *spiritual thoughts with spiritual words.*
>
> 1 Corinthians 2:11–13, italics added

Despite Paul's strong description and defense of the verbal nature of our spiritual life as Christians, the word *spiritual* is still a very abstract term—it is quite large and deep as a lexical bucket into which many meanings and mixtures can be and have been poured by other seekers of spiritual truth. That is certainly true in our pluralistic age, when being "spiritual" is a valued quality no matter what beliefs may shape a person's spirituality. But that was also true in other ways in the time of Jesus, which is why He so skillfully used illustrative language to help His followers make sense of His preaching of the gospel and other truths about the spiritual world He came to reveal.

Saying Kingdom Words

The gospel, or the "good news" of Jesus Christ, is the starting place for our spiritual lives as Christians, but to fully explore exactly what the gospel is, you'd have to read all 132 New Testament verses that mention the term. For most, Paul's summary explanation is the go-to passage—Christ died for our sins and was buried, and He was raised on the third day and appeared to many (see 1 Corinthians 15:1–8). That's all good, but it misses a less discussed emphasis by Jesus—the "gospel of the kingdom." In Matthew, Jesus proclaimed it to begin His ministry and, just before the cross, said it would testify of Him until the end of this age. In Mark, Jesus declares it to begin His ministry, saying, "the time is fulfilled." In Luke, Jesus declares it as His message that has superseded the Law and the Prophets. Jesus taught more about the kingdom of God than any other topic.

First-century Jews would've understood the language of the "gospel of the kingdom." The Greek term for gospel, *euangelion*, was commonly used to announce the reign of a new king. In their ears, Jesus' announcement was not just about something to believe, but a declaration that the story of God as their King was still being told. That was the good news! About six hundred years earlier, Israel had sinned and rejected God, bringing His judgment in the fall of Jerusalem, the destruction of the temple, and exile in Babylon. But Isaiah had prophesied then that God was still King, and that He would one day return to reign on the throne in Jerusalem and bring peace. Israel had waited, and now they heard Jesus proclaiming that "the time is fulfilled" for the kingdom to be restored—for God to reign again and bring His peace (*shalom*) to all the nations. But when the people of Israel realized that Jesus was not coming as a King who would provide deliverance from the oppression of Rome, they rejected and crucified Him. He was not the Messiah they wanted.

When He was taken to Pilate, the governor of Judea, Jesus told him, "My kingdom is not of this world." When Pilate asked, "So You are a king?" Jesus replied, "You say correctly that I am a king. For this I have been born, and for this I have come into the world, to testify to the truth. Everyone who is of the truth hears My voice" (John 18:36–37). Though Pilate found no guilt in Him, the Jewish leaders secured His crucifixion. Jesus' act of love and sacrifice, as He was crowned with thorns and enthroned on the cross, would bring true peace—not the peace of freedom from Rome by the sword, but the peace of freedom from sin by the Spirit. By His death and resurrection, when He comes to reign as King in our hearts, He brings the *spiritual* peace that we all long for. The gospel of the kingdom is about more than just us getting into heaven; it is the story of heaven getting into us. That's a spiritual story to tell your children.

Even though our children never lived under the reign of a king, they intuitively understood what *kingdom* means and could imagine what a perfect and powerful King would be like. From the many books that had shaped their imaginations, they knew about kings, kingdoms, thrones, swords, subjects, battles, and all the rest of kingdom lore. The language Jesus used made His spiritual message concrete for the Jews of His day, and it also makes it concrete for children in our day. If we want to help our children understand what it means to live a spiritual life in a way that will enable them to "see" that truth in their minds, then we need to tell God's story with conviction, compassion, and concrete language.

But kingdom is not just one story out of many that can form faith. It is *the* story. It is the metanarrative of our Christian faith, the overarching story that God is telling in all His words—the word of His revelation, the Bible, and the Word of His incarnation, Jesus. God's kingdom is what turns the spiritual abstractions of Christian faith into concrete beliefs. The root of the word *abstract* means "to be drawn apart," and of the word *concrete*, "to be grown together." Giving your children a Christian imagination enables them to pull into their minds the often drawn-apart and disconnected truths of Christianity, and grow them together into a unified whole, into a story. Sarah has often said that "words make worlds," and the words that tell the story of God's kingdom pull together the spiritual worlds of God's story in a way that enables children to see and understand. Imagination is the key to giving them words that are spiritual in a way that helps them to see themselves as part of God's story.

154

Words That Build Imagination

But the challenge for parents is not just to become better storytellers for their children. It's also about helping children perceive the meaning and messages in the stories about God's spiritual worlds by means of their maturing imaginations. Dictionary.com defines imagination as a faculty for "forming mental images or concepts of what is not actually present to the senses." And, we would add, for forming a faith that can see and believe in things not present to their senses, that never have been seen, or that do not now exist. Imagination is a mental muscle that needs to be exercised and strengthened no less than physical muscles. If neglected, a child's faith can too easily settle into a pattern of acquiescence to propositional truth and to Scripture only as a history lesson to be studied or a textbook of truth and doctrine to be learned. Poet and philosopher Henry David Thoreau said, "The question is not what you look at, but what you see."[1] Imagination is the faculty by which we can see what we believe. Faith without imagination is not blind, but it can be seeing-impaired.

Sarah, our first student of the Christian imagination, says that imagination is "that faculty by which we perceive meaning beyond the mere surface of things, by which we picture and believe in 'things hoped for . . . not seen.'" God, she says, "crafted the world to tell of his presence and made us in his image as artists, storytellers, and creators."[2] That image in us, the *imago dei*, is complex and mysterious, but at its roots it is the part of our human nature that tells us we are not rocks or animals—we can imagine our own existence, and our Creator's. We can believe or not believe in that Creator, but that choice itself is evidence that something outside of the material universe has enabled us to imagine that we can *have* a choice. We imagine; therefore, we are. And out of all that, we are moved to relate to one another, to share our beliefs, and to tell stories, all using words given to us by the Creator.

All of this raises a question: How, then, do I strengthen my child's mental muscle of imagination? It's easy to make the mistake of thinking that imagination—like inspiration—just happens, but that's not true. Like a muscle, imagination will become weaker or stronger depending on how it is fed and used. Madeleine L'Engle, author of *A Wrinkle in Time*, said, "All children are artists, and it is an indictment of our culture that so many of them lose their creativity, their unfettered imaginations, as they grow older."[3] We agree, and though we could talk about what weakens imagination in your child, we believe that a good proactive offense obviates the need to do that. Instead, we'll focus on some verbal aspects of imagination building.

Talking

The more you talk to and with your children, the better. But the challenge is to talk about meaningful topics. There are many relational positives to be gained by just small talk with your children, but the biggest imaginal advantage is the words—the vocabulary. A child's ability to imagine things beyond their own senses is directly related to the depth and breadth of their vocabulary. It takes little imagination to realize the impact of limited vocabulary on success in life, or on spiritual understanding. However, the more words there are in your child's vocabulary, the greater will be the scope and intensity of what they can imagine. The stronger their grasp of language, the richer will be their creativity and ability to wonder about spiritual things beyond the senses.

Telling

Telling is one-way talking. It is the essence of giving your words. As a parent, you need to tell stories to your children—real and imagined, allegories and analogies, with narrative and dialogue, with illustrations and anecdotes. Your purpose in such storytelling is not just practical, such as for entertaining, comfort, or discipline. Rather, it is mentoring, to model how to tell a story (or share an idea, opinion, or insight). You are demonstrating for them flow of thought, expression, creativity, vocabulary, and other elements of how to tell stories. But having observed, they need to practice it themselves. Invite them to tell you their own stories, or suggest a setting and characters and ask what story they would tell. It's in their own telling that the imagination muscle is strengthened.

Reading

Reading of any kind—aloud, alone, or along—is food for the imagination, but only if the reading material is well written, is meaningful, and uses good vocabulary. And yes, if you are selecting or suggesting the reading material, and you are reading aloud regularly to your children, then reading is a very effective form of giving your words. Good books can impact the imagination on numerous levels: the example of writing by an author who takes words and language seriously; a creative or imaginative concept that invites discussion; a topic that requires a higher level of thinking; a book that creates a world that you and your children can inhabit; a story with characters and topics that stimulate interest and discussion. Reading is a critical tool for imagination building.

Writing

Putting pen to paper (or fonts to screen) may not sound like giving your words, but that's probably because you're thinking about your child doing the writing. The real power of writing is, again, in the modeling of it to your children. Ask your children what they would like for you to write about, then give it your best shot, and read aloud to them what you write. This is giving your words. It doesn't matter how good your writing is; it matters that they see you expressing yourself through writing in a way that they can imitate and emulate. Depending on their age and writing level, ask them to write something for you that they will read (or to dictate it to you and you can write for them). The mental process of translating a story or idea in your brain into a permanent form on paper requires the exercise of imagination.

Poetry

Beautiful verse in the form of poetry can be a richly imaginative combination of telling, reading, writing, and the arts. It is the artistic use of words, rhyme, meter, structure, and thought that is not only literary and spoken artistry, but also the most complex form of literary expression—whether for the writing, the reading, or the recitation. Beyond the artistic aspects, it is also a testimony to the creative nature of God, who created language. You can give your words by selecting, reading aloud, and discussing beautiful poetry. The poetry you share will become your words, and it may be remembered for years. For strengthening imagination, though, there is no better exercise than writing your own poetry, reading it aloud, discussing it, and then inviting your children to do the same. Poetry is the pinnacle of imagination formulation.

Arts

The creative arts of art and music do not sound at first like "giving your words," and yet they provide a rich medium for doing just that, and for unleashing and strengthening your children's imaginations. Model for your children how to enjoy a piece of art or music, and the kinds of questions you can ask about it—what the artist was trying to say, how it makes you feel, what makes it beautiful. The verbal appreciation and discussion of art for its creativity, beauty, and meaning can create stimulating moments of word-giving and also exercise the imaginations of your children. The more you practice this form of giving your words, the more your children will learn to recognize and value good art, and even desire to try it themselves with their own imaginations.

Keep in mind a few parting thoughts about imagination building. First, remember that imagination is not limited only to certain personality types. Some children may seem to possess a larger *capacity* for imagination than others, but all children share the same *capability* for it. Every child is made in God's image and is invested with the same God-given imagination that needs to be exercised and developed. Second, imagination is not learned from a workbook or manual. It is grown and cultivated at home in a words-rich environment and atmosphere. Good things grow in good soil, which includes imaginations in the soil of a verbally enriched Christian home.

Finally, giving your children words that are spiritual is not the same as teaching them spiritual words. The purpose of using words to strengthen their imaginations is to form their faith to not only believe in the spiritual *words* of the Bible, but to also see themselves in the spiritual *worlds* that those words reveal. Recalling C. S. Lewis's toolshed moment, it is not just looking *at* but *along* the words in order to see the worlds. You are forming their faith to follow Paul's admonition: "Therefore if you have been raised up with Christ, keep seeking the things above, where Christ is, seated at the right hand of God. Set your mind on the things above, not on the things that are on earth" (Colossians 3:1–2). Knowledge about the spiritual world, without the ability to perceive and conceive what that world is like, is just words in a travel guide for a country you only read about. Giving your children spiritual words for their growing imaginations will provide the map for their own spiritual journeys.

Imagination in the Bible

You may think that talking about your children's imagination is not really a biblical concept, but Jesus affirmed the faith of children, and the apostle Paul affirms imagination as an aspect of faith. He prays for the Ephesian believers that God would give them "the Spirit of wisdom and revelation, so that you may know [Christ] better" (1:17 NIV). Literally, he wants their knowledge to be precise and correct, and goes on to explain what he means:

> I pray that *the eyes of your heart may be enlightened* in order that *you may know* the hope to which he has called you, the riches of his glorious inheritance in his holy people, and his incomparably great power for us who believe. That power is the same as the mighty strength he exerted when he raised Christ from the dead and seated him at his right hand *in the heavenly realms.*
>
> 1:18–20 NIV, italics added

Paul prays that the Holy Spirit would shine a light in the Ephesians' imaginations so they could see with spiritual eyes what they could not see with their physical eyes. The "eyes of your heart" is simply an analogy for the imagination, and light is a symbol of God's truth. He prays that they would not just know *about* these things intellectually, but know them *by experience (eido)*—all that God has done and is doing "in the heavenly realms," the great story He is telling through the incarnated, resurrected, and glorified Christ. Paul is giving them words that are spiritual so the Ephesian believers would be able to "see" themselves in those spiritual worlds. And that is what you are doing by giving your children words that are spiritual.

The prophet Isaiah, speaking to Jews who hoped in God's covenant promises to Israel, said, "The steadfast of mind You will keep in perfect peace, because he trusts in You" (26:3). Or, literally, "The steadfast of imagination (*yatsar*)" the LORD GOD would keep in His *shalom*. The prophet is speaking to the one who can imagine "that day" when God, the One on Whom Israel had waited for deliverance, "will swallow up death for all time, and the Lord GOD will wipe tears from all faces" (Isaiah 25:8). He tells Israel to imagine what is true beyond what their rational minds tell them, and to envision with hope spiritual realities and worlds that God has promised.

The author of the book of Hebrews also affirms the imagination and hope when he says, "Now faith is the assurance of things hoped for, the conviction of things not seen" (11:1). In other words, our hope is based on a firm belief in things we cannot confirm by our physical senses. Paul affirms the same thing, saying "hope that is seen is not hope; for who hopes for what he already sees?" (Romans 8:24). Our hope, of course, is that after death we will live eternally with God "in the heavenly realms." The truths you believe about death and eternal life will enter your children's imaginations only as they move into young adulthood. If their imaginations and faith have been biblically formed and informed during childhood, then their maturing faith will be comfortable in the spiritual words they have heard and worlds they have already learned to envision.

Spiritual Worlds of the Imagination

We've asked more of you as a parent in this chapter than is typical of most parenting "how to" books. Our goal has not been simply to give you things to do with and say to your children, but rather to give you a higher calling as a Christian parent. We have just barely scratched the surface of giving words that are spiritual, only because Scripture is a wholly spiritual book—every page requires imagination and faith to understand and believe its stories, histories, truths, tales, teachings, promises, people, and prophecies. From Genesis to Revelation, it is an unfolding spiritual account of our origins, purpose, and destiny—where we came from, why we are here, and where we are going. It is the story of our Creator becoming a man in order to die for our sins and overcome death so that we can live forever with Him. There is literally nothing in the Bible that can be reduced for children to "just a story"—it is *all* about spiritual words and worlds. As parents, we made it our purpose not to hide those realties from our children, but to invite our children into the spiritual journey that we were on.

To close this chapter, we want to offer one more acrostic that we hope will help simplify the spiritual words you give to your children to open their imaginations to the spiritual worlds that God is giving to us. The acrostic, formed by the word WORLDS, is admittedly insufficient even as an attempted summary, but it will at least give you a starting point to help you know what kinds of spiritual words to give your children along the way.

- W: Word—Giving words that are spiritual to your children begins with the Bible, the God-breathed (*theopneustos*) word of the eternal God to us (2 Timothy 3:15–16), and Jesus, the incarnated Word (*Logos*) who brought us life and light (John 1:1–5). Spiritual words also include our words of wisdom, given to us from the Holy Spirit, given to our children. All that we know about the spiritual nature of this world is in God's word. The life in the Spirit that we want to give to our children must begin and end in the words of Scripture.

- O: Order—God created the heavens and the earth (Genesis 1:1) through Jesus (Colossians 1:16). The order and structure of the physical universe is a testimony to the God of order who created it—it didn't happen by random chance or accident. Spiritual worlds created by God will exhibit the same order—they are not chaotic, and we can believe what God says about them. God is not a God of disorder (1 Corinthians 14:33).

- R: Real—Most Christian children are engaged at some level with fantasy books, media, and games, so it is important to distinguish between images—visual or literary—that distort biblical reality and those that attempt to accurately reflect what is described in Scripture. Most important is to present the Bible's spiritual truths about the spirit world as real. We can imagine how things might be, but not whether or not they really exist.

- L: Light—The defining qualities of the spiritual world in which God resides are light and life. If you recall from earlier, that is also the nature of God's grace, His spiritual gift to us that brings us joy. The spiritual absence of light and life is darkness and death (John 1:4–5). But scripture proclaims, "This is the message we have heard from Him . . . that God is Light, and in Him there is no darkness at all" (1 John 1:5). We can walk in His Light.

- D: Dark—Perhaps all that needs to be said here is Ephesians 6:12: "For our struggle is not against flesh and blood, but against the rulers, against the powers, against the world forces of this darkness, against the spiritual forces of wickedness in the heavenly places." Spiritual darkness cannot be ignored, but Christ's light overcomes the dark.

- S: Spirit—Tell your children that the Holy Spirit living within us is our spiritual power for living for God: "If we live by the Spirit, let us also walk by the Spirit" (Galatians 5:25). Tell them it is by the Spirit that we are spiritual people: "The Spirit Himself testifies with our spirit that we are children of God" (Romans 8:16). Tell them our spiritual destiny is secure: "You were sealed in [Christ] with the Holy Spirit of promise" (Ephesians 1:13).

— • —

If, as Sarah says, words make worlds, then begin building the spiritual worlds in your children's minds that will prepare them to live with faith and hope as mature and spiritual Christian adults when they leave your home. Become a spiritual mentor, modeling for them what it means to live in the power of the Holy Spirit—to "walk in the Light as He Himself is in the Light" (1 John 1:7), to "put on the full armor of God, so that you will be able to stand firm against the schemes of the devil" (Ephesians 6:11), and to "press on toward the goal for the prize of the upward call of God in Christ Jesus" (Philippians 3:14). Be the spiritual person you want your children to become, and give them the words they need so that they too will "be strong in the grace that is in Christ Jesus" (2 Timothy 2:1).

Parenting
VERBALOGISTICS

There are few better ways to stimulate your children's imaginations and give them spiritual words and ideas at the same time than by reading aloud THE CHRONICLES OF NARNIA, C. S. Lewis's seven-book allegory of the Christian life written for children but loved by all ages. The entire series delighted our children numerous times. Not only is it good children's literature, but each book will provide opportunities to talk about a variety of spiritual topics. A good companion book that explores the allegorical features of the Narnia books with family discussion suggestions is *A Family Guide to Narnia*, by Christin Ditchfield. Set aside a special time to read the CHRONICLES out loud together as a family. If your children are young, reward them after reading with the BBC video series first released in 1988, which is very low-tech, but high in fidelity to the books. The stories and images from Narnia will become a natural part of your spiritual thinking. Later, when your children are a bit older, you can also enjoy John Bunyan's classic allegory of the Christian life, *The Pilgrim's Progress*. Though Bunyan wrote his story for adults, we enjoyed reading *Dangerous Journey* with our children, an abridged version of the story using Bunyan's own words and illustrated vividly with visual re-creations of scenes from Christian's journey. The stories, allegories, and analogies will shape how you and your children think about the Christian life.

EIGHT

Words That Are Wisdom

Be very careful, then, how you live—not as unwise but as wise, making the most of every opportunity, because the days are evil.

Ephesians 5:15–16 NIV

An oft-quoted biblical proverb in our home was about wisdom and relationships: "He who walks with wise men will be wise, but the companion of fools will suffer harm" (13:20). In other words, wisdom is learned from the wise, and its absence in others can be dangerous. It's a top-ten teen years verse, but we applied it to more than just our children's choices of friends. We let them know that we, their parents, were the "wise people" they should want to walk with to gain wisdom from our words. We were confident, as we walked with God alongside our children, that they would become wise as we brought them up in the training and instruction of the Lord (see Ephesians 6:4).

We made sure our children walked with us whenever possible—local errands, church meetings, seeing friends, ministry events, national conferences, international mission trips—observing us in real life and hearing our instruction and words all along the way. But it was Sally who made that family "walk-and-talk" into a special time of discipleship with our girls. Sally started her Saturday morning walks when we moved to Monument in 1999, when Sarah was fifteen and Joy was just four. Moving across the country to a new city would be a challenging time for any young teen girl, but our lifestyle of homeschooling and a growing national family ministry hadn't made it easy for Sarah to make friends her age. So every Saturday morning, weather permitting, Sally would be Sarah's friend, taking her for a walk-and-talk in Colorado Springs. The twenty-two-mile drive from our house in the Monument foothills to downtown gave them even more relaxed time together as they listened to favorite music and casually chatted in the car.

Their first destination was always La Baguette, a French bakery and espresso bar on a quiet side street in the heart of downtown. As light classical music played softly in the background, they would enjoy strong coffee and a freshly baked breakfast croissant. Sally always had gentle questions tucked away in her mind to ask Sarah that would draw her out to discover how she was feeling about her new life in the Springs, and about her faith. But she also always came to those times with biblical wisdom and insights she was ready to share with Sarah. She considered it a strategic time of personal discipleship with her oldest child, following the "with Him" discipleship modeled by Jesus as she built a loving relationship and helped Sarah understand the Christian life. And though they were sitting, Sally was nonetheless walking with Sarah figuratively, as one who would help her become a wise and godly woman. After breakfast, they would continue their walk-and-talk along the sidewalks of the Old North End on streets lined with lovely old Victorian homes. Those casual mother-daughter times helped Sarah navigate the changes and challenges of her young life.

After a two-year family and ministry detour to Tennessee, and a return to Monument in 2004, Joy would join the Colorado walk-and-talk times when she was around ten years old. For a few years, before Sarah would leave home, it was a "girls' club." Then, as Joy became a teen, Sally would use the walk-and-talk as she had done with Sarah to build her relationship with Joy and disciple her in her walk with the Lord. There were also "Girls' Nights Out," and times of celebration when words of wisdom were shared—receiving gold rings at thirteen as a reminder to stay pure and committed to Christ, and receiving special Bibles and gifts at sixteen as they prepared for a new season of life. Sally was teaching and talking with Sarah and Joy simply as a way of lifegiving—giving them wisdom from the word and her words to find God's way for their walks in the world with the wind of the Spirit at their backs.

The Walk of Parental Wisdom

Growing in wisdom is the long game of giving your words as a parent to your children. As you walk with them as they grow and mature through childhood and young adulthood, you are giving them words that will be the building blocks of wisdom in their hearts and minds. You cannot train a child to have wisdom, as though it is a distinct capability such as obedience, diligence, or self-control. Wisdom is not a character quality. However, through training and instruction with the Lord, you can prepare their hearts to receive Christ and the wisdom He gives. Under the old covenant, wisdom was gained by combining godly knowledge with life experience. Under the new covenant, true wisdom is found only in Christ and the Holy Spirit. Your words are preparing the soil of your child's heart to receive the seed of the word of God, which is the gospel of Christ, so that they will "hold it fast, and bear fruit with perseverance" (Luke 8:15). The long game of giving your words is to see your children receive Christ and begin living by the power of the Holy Spirit, who will use those words to direct them, as they live by faith, to walk in the way of God's wisdom.

This chapter is not about giving your children words that will make them wise, but about words that will strengthen their wisdom muscle, that will give them what Paul describes as "a spirit of wisdom" (Ephesians 1:17). We've seen a variety of "parenting with Proverbs" books, but memorizing and quoting Proverbs alone will not make your child wise. Proverbs can help your child learn *how* to think but not *what* to think. "For wisdom will enter your heart and knowledge will be pleasant to your soul; discretion will guard you, understanding will watch over you" (2:10). In other words, wisdom is like a spiritual muscle with which they will apply knowledge, discretion, and understanding. Proverbs are helpful, but they are only a means, not the end, to the wisdom you want your child to have, which is the wisdom that comes from the Holy Spirit.

The biblical topic of wisdom is vast, but to try to create some graspable handles, we will take advantage of some agreeably alliterative English words to focus our thoughts. You may have missed it at the end of the story above, but this chapter is about giving your children *wisdom* from the *word* and your *words* to find God's *way* for their *walk* in this *world* by the *wind* of the Spirit. These will be, switching metaphors now, very small bites of the very large apple of wisdom, but hopefully it will be enough to whet your appetite to study wisdom more. If you start with the truth that all wisdom begins in God, then you'll stay on the right path: "The fear of the LORD is the beginning of wisdom" (Psalm 111:10; Proverbs 9:10).

Wisdom

Wisdom has its own books in the Old Testament, so that's where we'll start. More than two-thirds of the Hebrew words for wisdom (*hakma*) and wise (*hakam*) are in three books— Job, Proverbs, and Ecclesiastes—comprising less than one-half of one percent of the Hebrew Bible's 622,700 words. We typically think of Proverbs as the "wisdom book" of the Bible with advice for living skillfully. Proverbs, though, are not prescriptive truths meant to be obeyed, but rather are pithy precepts of divine wisdom meant to be considered— counsel, not commands; principles, not promises; directives, not imperatives. In that way they are similar to the parables of Jesus. Wisdom writers and sages taught about living wisely by choosing between good and evil, righteousness and wickedness, and wisdom and folly.

Proverbs are written primarily for youth and adults; there are no little children mentioned in the book. Proverbs can be useful for children, but they are not formulations of divine wisdom that will somehow make them wise. The wise person of Proverbs is not instructed to claim them, but to listen to them, learn from them, apply them, and grow in godly discernment and wisdom. You should give proverbs to your children with the same view in mind—to help teach them what it means to think with discernment and understanding as they become young men and young women. Proverbs will not make them wise, but can contribute to their becoming spiritually mature as they follow Christ and live by the Spirit.

Looking forward into the New Testament, though, the possibility of a godly life offered by the wisdom of Proverbs is part of the Law-keeping life that will be nailed to the cross. True wisdom from God is fully realized only with the coming of Jesus and the life of the Holy Spirit in the believer. Jesus closed His Sermon on the Mount by claiming that His words are the foundation of wisdom—the one who "hears these words of Mine and acts on them, may be compared to a wise man who built his house on the rock" (Matthew 7:24). Paul will go on to teach that Jesus is the embodiment of God's wisdom, and our wisdom will come from being "in Christ Jesus, who became to us wisdom from God" (1 Corinthians 1:30). Wisdom is no longer the Law-like external instructions of Proverbs to be mastered for godly living, but rather the internal presence and work of the Holy Spirit giving us a new heart and spirit of wisdom from God. Paul said his messages "were not in persuasive words of wisdom, but in demonstration of the Spirit and of power, so that your faith would not rest on the wisdom of men, but on the power of God" (1 Corinthians 2:4–5). If you want to give wise words to your children that will form their faith, those words will come from the Holy Spirit in you as a believer. Your verbal goal as a words-giving parent is to be like Paul, "admonishing and teaching everyone with all wisdom, so that we may present everyone fully mature in Christ" (Colossians 1:28 NIV).

We'll let James have the last word on wisdom. His letter is like a taste of Proverbs in the New Testament, and yet James clearly rejects finding one's righteousness in the "works" of keeping rules and laws. He asserts that true wisdom comes by faith: "If any of you lacks wisdom, you should ask God, who gives generously to all without finding fault, and it will be given to you" (1:5 NIV). He also argues that true wisdom is demonstrated by godly character: "Who is wise and understanding among you? Let them show it by their good life, by deeds done in the humility that comes from wisdom" (3:13 NIV). God's wisdom is not about worldly arguments and disputes, James says, but "is first of all pure; then peace-loving, considerate, submissive, full of mercy and good fruit, impartial and sincere" (3:17 NIV). The words of wisdom you give to your children should emphasize faith in God as the wisdom Giver and heavenly source of "every good and perfect gift" (1:17), and they should affirm good and godly character that shows love and results in peace. In other words, true wisdom looks like Jesus.

Word

We took a deep dive into "the word of God" in the opening chapter, but it bears another look here through the lens of wisdom. Poetical and wisdom books of the Bible—Job, Psalms, Proverbs, Ecclesiastes—speak of the "word of God" and the "word of the LORD" with a variety of terms, but perhaps nowhere as fully as in Psalm 119, the longest chapter in Scripture. The word of God is referenced in 171 of its 176 verses with eight distinctive Hebrew words. The tone and wording of this psalm reflect the first-person narrative of the Psalms, but also the discreet instructive content of Proverbs. As an acrostic poem, Psalm 119 has been described as a string of pearls rather than as a chain of thought. With each of its twenty-two stanzas of eight verses, each beginning with a letter of the Hebrew alphabet, it was designed to be memorized like other wisdom literature. Like Proverbs chapters 1–9, it is a beautifully crafted piece of Hebraic poetic wisdom.

The book of Proverbs, however, is distinctively practical. A definition of Proverbs' wisdom could be "living wisely and righteously to please the Lord and enjoy His favor." The Mosaic Law is a subtext to what it means to live righteously (to choose the way of righteousness), but with only a few exceptions, none of the words referring to the "word of God" in Psalm 119 are used in Proverbs. There is a down-to-earthness about the book that keeps Proverbs focused more on practical matters of life and living than on propositional points of divine qualities and theology.

Those thoughts are at best just a few small pieces of marble in a large and complex biblical mosaic about wisdom and God's word. Still, there is something that can be learned for the parental task of giving words of wisdom to your children from God's word. It's about application. But we don't mean the too-often forced or artificial Bible study or devotional application. Rather, our conviction is that the most biblical application for any study of Scripture is prayer—not doing something *for* God but speaking *to* God, responding to the words He has given by talking with Him about them. It is in that divine-human dialogue that the Holy Spirit will impress on your children's hearts and yours how a scripture can apply to your lives with a change of heart, mind, or behavior.

All of Scripture teaches us how to live (see 2 Timothy 3:15–16), so it is important to train your children how to let individual Scripture passages and verses guide their lives and decisions, not as "proof texts" to apply without thinking, but as wisdom. That's why your first priority should be to train your children how to *think* about scriptures they read. One useful application model that combines prayer *and* action is what we call our "Faith FourWords" outline. When you read a scripture, simply ask, "Is there something in this scripture that God wants me to know, be, do, or believe?" That "know-be-do-believe" question can be asked of any verse or passage you and your children read in God's inspired word. It is a way of learning to hear the words that God is giving to you in His word.

Words

We always enjoyed reading Proverbs because they could easily lead to discussions about character, virtue, habits, disciplines, and choices. The wisdom was not always just in the words of the proverb, but in the principles it would suggest. When Joel was around ten years old, he and Sally had a devotional time together from a familiar passage in Proverbs: "Go to the ant, you sluggard; consider its ways and be wise!" (Proverbs 6:6 NIV). Joel was not being sluggardly, but the passage prompted a good discussion about responsibility, discipline, and diligence. Sally used the principles in the passage to give Joel her own words about those areas of personal character. The next day, without being asked or directed, Joel initiated a project on his own to organize two dozen heavy boxes of books in our storage area. He was not "obeying" a proverb, but simply taking words of wisdom from Scripture, given to him by his mother, and putting them into practice. That's how wisdom works.

A biblical example of that process is in Proverbs itself, in Solomon's words to his children. Numerous times in the first seven chapters he personalizes his appeal to them: "Hear, my son, *your father's instruction* and do not forsake *your mother's teaching*" (1:8, italics added). Solomon referring to the personal wisdom they offered is reminiscent of Moses instructing parents to use God's words impressed on their hearts to "sharpen" their children by talking of them repeatedly, which would mean discussing how to live wisely by God's word. And perhaps we can see it in the life of Jesus, described by Luke both as a child and a boy, as "increasing in wisdom." It seems to indicate that Jesus, even as the Son of God, was growing in wisdom, at least in part because He lived in a home where words from Joseph and Mary were given that contributed to that aspect of His nature as both God and man.

You have words that are wisdom to give to your children that are born out of your own life experience, successes and failures, walk in the Spirit, and knowledge of God's word. Your own godly wisdom, shaped by your relationship with Jesus and the Spirit within you, can be just as important to give to your children as the actual words of Scripture. Solomon told his children that he had acquired wisdom from his father, David, and that as a parent he had grown in wisdom that he could then give to them. He had been down the road they were on and could give them the wisdom to walk the "path of the righteous" wisely and safely. He is confident that the words of wisdom he gives to them, his counsel and advice, will keep them on God's path of life. You can be confident to follow Solomon's example with your own children and say as he did, "I have directed you in the way of wisdom; I have led you in upright paths" (Proverbs 4:11). That's the role of giving your words.

Way

The way of life—also path of life, way of wisdom, way of the righteous, way of the Lord—is a universally recognized metaphor for both Jews and Christians of the way to live faithfully with God. "Way" envisions a journey marked by choosing between life and blessing on "the way of wisdom," and death and curse on "the way of the wicked" (see Proverbs 4:10–19). In the Old Testament, the choice was made clear at the reading of the Law: "I have set before you life and death, the blessing and the curse. So choose life in order that you may live" (Deuteronomy 30:19). In the poetical and wisdom literature, that choice is expressed as the "way of life," of living wisely by God's laws and precepts. But through Jeremiah God declares, "I will put My law within them and on their heart I will write it" (31:33), and in Ezekiel He says, "I will give you a new heart and put a new spirit within you" (36:26). The prophets saw the coming of the Messiah and the work of the Holy Spirit that would provide a new way of life. Pastor and author Eugene Peterson said, "The Way that is Jesus cannot be reduced to information or instruction. The Way is a person whom we believe and follow as

God-with-us."[1] Jesus would not only *provide* a new way of life, but He would *be* that Way of life.

Jesus would declare himself to be the "way of the Lord" when He claimed, "I am the way, and the truth, and the life; no one comes to the Father but through Me" (John 14:6). As the embodiment of "the way," His truth and His life would provide what the prophets had foreseen. And after His ascension, the new church would so closely identify with Jesus' claim that they would be known as "the Way." Before his conversion, Paul (then Saul) had authority "if he found any belonging to the Way" (Acts 9:2) to arrest them, but twenty years later he would respond to accusations by Jewish leaders "that according to the Way which they call a sect I do serve the God of our fathers" (Acts 24:14).

When you give your children words of wisdom, whether from the Old or the New Testament, the "way of life" you are directing them to is not just learning wise words to help them make good decisions and stay out of trouble. Those can certainly be good words to give to them, but they will be words without the real truth and life your children need if they are given apart from Jesus and the Spirit. To give your children wisdom for the way of life, you need first to give them the real Way of life: Jesus. That's what the next three handles are about.

Walk

At least three things should be true about a path: It has a destination, you'll get there by walking, and you should look up and ahead. We discovered early on, from living near and walking on many mountain paths, that it's all too easy to look down at your feet when you're on a trail, mostly out of an overly cautious fear of stumbling. But we learned that it's better to look up and ahead to where you're going, not only to make sure you get there, but also to enjoy the scenery on the path and the people walking with you. The point of the spiritual metaphor is that the whole reason for being on a path is to walk and to reach a destination. But what, you may be asking, does walking have to do with giving words? That becomes clearer in the New Testament, where walking becomes an extended metaphor not just of life with God, but of living and maturing as a disciple of Jesus Christ. In that context, giving your words becomes about applying Jesus' Great Commission mandate to your home—to make disciples of your children by teaching them what it means to follow Christ (see Matthew 28:18–20). We believe Christian parenting is a discipleship ministry.

The apostle Paul, in his letter to the Colossian church, paints a beautiful word picture of discipleship as walking with Christ when he encourages believers to "walk in a manner worthy of the Lord, to please Him in all respects, bearing fruit in every good work and increasing in the knowledge of God" (1:10), then reminding them, "Therefore, as you have received Christ Jesus the Lord, so walk in Him" (2:6). It is certainly a picture of what we want for our children, so giving our words adds the lines and colors of being a disciple of Christ to the concepts of biblical wisdom we want to place in their hearts and minds.

We are walking on the Old Testament "path of wisdom" with our children, but as Christians, the destination has changed from avoiding darkness and death to becoming like Jesus—who is the Way—to find light and life in Him.

In our family, walking on the path of life with our children was about giving them direction (to stay on the path), correction (to bring them back to the path), and protection (to guard them from temptations off the path). Each of those verbal activities is an intensive word-giving and heart-to-heart interaction. It becomes discipleship as we speak words to form and inform their developing faith so they will live for Christ and walk by faith with Him.

The process of helping your children walk as young disciples of Jesus is the same as what Luke said of the young Jesus: "The Child continued to grow and to become strong, increasing in wisdom; and the favor of God was upon Him" (2:40). As your children grow older and become physically stronger, they will also be growing in spiritual and personal wisdom, just as Jesus did. And God's grace will be upon them because of the words of truth and wisdom you give to them as you walk in faith with them. They will be like Timothy, who from infancy, Paul said, had known the sacred writings (the Old Testament), which were able to give him "the wisdom that leads to salvation through faith which is in Christ Jesus" (2 Timothy 3:15). Timothy heard the words of God's wisdom even from the womb. Discipleship is a lifelong walk on the path of life with your children.

World

The "way of the wicked" in the Old Testament wisdom literature becomes the "world" in the New Testament. Not the physical world that God made through Jesus (Hebrews 1:2), or the spiritual world in which we follow "the Light of the world" (John 8:12), or the lost and broken world that "God so loved" (John 3:16). Rather, the "way of the wicked" is the world system in which "people loved the darkness more than the light, for their actions were evil" (John 3:19 NLT). The world is not evil, since God made it and called it good, but evil is in the world since the fall, and now "the whole world is under the control of the evil one" (1 John 5:19 NIV). But wisdom still provides the many biblical signposts that keep the followers of God on the path of light, life, and good, rather than the path of darkness, death, and evil. Wisdom is still a choice of good rather than evil.

But how do you give words that are wisdom to your children about that choice before they reach young adulthood? Young children know the difference between right and wrong, but they are innocent in the knowledge of good and evil (see Deuteronomy 1:39). If you make them fearful of the evil world system too soon—an abstraction beyond their grasp—they will learn to fear the darkness but not to love the light. Instead, as we said earlier from Jesus' parable of the sower, give words of wisdom that will cultivate in your child an "honest and good heart" that can value and recognize the goodness of God. Stay focused on Jesus, the "light of the world" who gives the "light of life" (John 8:12 NIV). As they turn the corner into their teen years, you can focus more on how to "not love the world nor the things in the world" (1 John 2:15) and how to "not be conformed to this world" (Romans 12:2).

There is a "wisdom of this world [that] is foolishness before God" (1 Corinthians 3:19), and your children will be exposed to it simply because they are living in this world. If you're not sure how you can counter that influence, take James's advice: "But if any of you lacks wisdom, let him ask of God who gives to all generously and without reproach, and it will be given to him" (1:5). When it comes to navigating the darkness of this world as a parent with young children, walk in the light given by Jesus, "the Light of the world," and you will find the words of wisdom you need to give to them.

Wind (Spirit)

This final handle for grasping the biblical topic of wisdom is a spiritual metaphor. Without it, wisdom as a faculty is limited to fallen human reason; with it, wisdom is the supernatural power of God working in you. The wind of wisdom is the Holy Spirit. Nicodemus, a Jewish religious leader, met with Jesus under cover of darkness to ask about His teaching. When Jesus said, "Unless one is born again he cannot see the kingdom of God" (John 3:3), Nicodemus didn't understand. Jesus explained that even though one sees the effects of the wind, no one knows where it came from or where it is going. As with the wind (*pneuma*), Jesus said, so it is with everyone born of the Spirit (*pneuma*). It is a supernatural influence. When the wind of the Holy Spirit is blowing through you and your family, God's wisdom will be felt by everyone in your home. Your words can be words of spiritual wisdom for your children.

Dr. Lawrence Richards makes the wisdom choice clear: "Only when one abandons what seems wise by human standards to accept without hesitation the divine viewpoint as revealed in Scripture can he claim true wisdom."[2] That "divine viewpoint" comes from the Holy Spirit. The apostle Paul explains how the Spirit works: "What we have received is not the *spirit of the world*, but the *Spirit who is from God*, so that we may understand what God has freely given us. This is what we *speak*, not in *words* taught us by human wisdom but in words taught *by the Spirit*, explaining spiritual realities with Spirit-taught words" (1 Corinthians 2:12–13 NIV, italics added). If you have received the "Spirit who is from God," you have the supernatural power working in you to give your children "words taught by the Spirit." Your challenge as a parent, then, is to follow Paul's advice to the Galatians: "If we live by the Spirit, let us also walk by the Spirit" (5:25). Study the scriptures to learn how to walk by the Spirit so you will have spiritual thoughts and spiritual words to give to your children.

— • —

Giving your children words that are wisdom—words that will become a spirit of wisdom in them by the Spirit of God—will probably be the most "spiritual" thing you do as a parent. You may not feel that spiritual, or think that you have spiritual words to give, but the biblical reality is that both are true by the presence of the Holy Spirit within you. When you come to accept that reality, though, you will be faced with another: Time is short. Remember Proverbs 13:20, "He who walks with wise men will be wise." You have only a small window of time to walk with your children to give them words of wisdom needed to walk with God as adults. To be those "wise people" for your children, you need to make the most of this time.

The apostle Paul challenged the Ephesian believers with the same reality that you face. "Be very careful, then, how you live—not as unwise but as wise, making the most of every opportunity, because the days are evil" (5:15–16 NIV). Let Paul's words speak to you as a parent. He admonishes the Ephesians to diligently take heed how they are walking. Take the time to evaluate your spiritual life. Then, understand the metaphor Paul uses to challenge you to live wisely by "redeeming the time" (NKJV), picturing the act of purchasing time out of slavery to the world and setting it free. Finally, realize that the "time" being set free is your *kairos*, your season of opportune time. In other words, it is right now. You have words that are wisdom to give to your children, so seize the *kairos*!

Parenting
VERBALOGISTICS

The book of Proverbs is filled with pithy wisdom that can fuel many great family discussions. The Hebrew word for *wisdom* includes the idea of skill, so Proverbs is arguably a primer on skillful living, with lots to discuss. However, searching through eight hundred proverbs to find the ones you want to talk about can be a daunting task. So here's a family project. Whether you do it on paper or on a computer, create your own "Proverbs Project Wisdom Workbook." Just start reading through Proverbs as a family and putting them in categories. If you can, we suggest you photocopy or print out all of the Proverbs one-sided onto copy paper and put the sheets into a three-ring binder. Use colored markers or pencils, or your own category codes to mark the verses. Take it a chapter at a time as a family to work your way through the book. You can create your own topical categories, or use the suggested "living skillfully" outline below for your Wisdom Workbook:

TEN WORDS OF WISDOM

Personal

Skillful with Trust (faith, fear of God)
Skillful with Truth (integrity, truth, lies)
Skillful with Discernment (fools, folly, wisdom)
Skillful with Self (anger, pride, envy)
Skillful with Choices (good and evil, way of life, blessings)

Practical

Skillful with Words (mouth, tongue)
Skillful with Money (wealth, debt, poverty)
Skillful with Living (health, happiness, life)
Skillful with Labor (work, diligence)
Skillful with Discipline (discipline, correction, children)

NINE

Words That Are Believable

Faith shows the reality of what we hope for; it is the evidence of things we cannot see.

Hebrews 11:1 NLT

When our children were all younger and in need of being shuttled between classes, lessons, events, and friends, there were many miles of captive audience car time that got filled with fun talks, singing songs together, or just chilling. However, we were also sensitive to those hours on the road being opportunities to talk about faith.

In general, we filtered news whenever we could, but one day a news story about bad people stirred up a conversation about God and Satan. After Sally shared some biblical thoughts and asked a few questions, preschooler Joel was quiet and obviously pensive. Finally, carefully forming his ideas, he posed a question: "Mommy, if God is good, and Satan is evil, how could a good God make a bad Satan?"

Hearing questions like that one delighted us because we knew we were listening to the forging of belief in the furnace of the heart and mind. There would be many years of words to fully define those biblical beliefs, but the process of deciding and believing what is real had begun.

How many times have you told your child a wonderful story only to hear them ask, "Is that a real story?" It belies, at least a little, the common claim that children will believe anything you tell them. Still, though less discerning about what is really true, they are no less desirous of believing in the believability of what they are told is true. Like the rest of us, if they learn that they've been tricked, they will become skeptical and guarded. When you talk with your children about biblical stories and truths, many of them can seem completely unbelievable on some level, maybe even leaving you to ponder privately where suspending disbelief ends and believing by faith begins. And if that's true for you, then it can be true in a less sophisticated way for your children, too.

Giving words that are believable means confidently sharing what you have chosen to believe by faith. Your assurance of those given words will provide spiritual anchors for your children that will keep the ship of their own faith from drifting as they enter young adulthood. What we call family faith formation is a two-pronged process—it is the "family faith" that you bring as parents to the formation of your child's spirit; and it is the "faith formation" that happens only in the context of a loving and faith-full family.[1]

Typically, discussions about childhood faith tend to be reduced to child-friendly "believe and be saved" salvation appeals. However, there is much more to childhood faith than meets the "I believe." Remember, Jesus considered a young child's faith just as valid as an adult's (see Matthew 18:1–6). The faith/believe word family is number four on the list of most frequently used words in the New Testament, its 501 occurrences exceeded only by *God*, *Jesus*, and *Lord*.[2] Obviously, faith is a complex biblical topic with many facets beyond just the propositional transaction of "saving faith." That's why we chose not to "evangelize" our children, but rather to train and instruct them in faith and immerse them in our faith-filled home. Nineteenth-century British pastor and author Andrew Murray also affirmed that dynamic: "Faith was not only to be solely a personal thing but an act that embraced the household and then flowed out to enclose every family member."[3]

There are far more facets and facts of faith in the New Testament than we can cover in a few pages here, so this chapter will focus narrowly on some examples of how family dynamics can cultivate biblical faith in your children. In our experience, family faith formation is primarily verbal, so our interest will be on the special role of words in creating an immersive atmosphere of grace and faith in your home.

Believing in the Words You Give

Every Christian family discovers its own preferred way to have family devotions—a time to gather, read the Bible aloud, talk about the story or passage, and pray together as a family. There is no "right way" to do that other than the way it happens best and most consistently for your family. In our home, the natural time for family devotions was at the family table after breakfast—when the day was just getting started, everyone was rested and fresh, and cereal or eggs filled happy stomachs and fueled good discussion. We rarely used a prepared devotional, but rather would read through a book of the Bible or selected scriptures about a topic of interest. Occasionally, we might read from a book and talk about scriptures related to what the author had to say, or just read an extract of writing and let it lead us naturally into the Scripture. We preferred an organic approach to devotions, letting them grow naturally from the soil of our family life. As with all things when young children are in the home, those morning devotions were unpredictable. No matter where the discussions about the day's scripture might lead—lively repartee, varying opinions, unexpectedly cogent insights, rambling rabbit trails, humorous biblical malapropisms, or the infrequent awkward silence—our goal was never to elicit "right answers" but always to stimulate and cultivate biblical thinking and verbal processing. We wanted our children to feel the freedom to say whatever they were thinking without the fear of saying something "wrong." We asked questions in a child-friendly, Socratic way that helped them think critically about their responses and opinions, trusting that right answers would grow from the organics of our verbal interactions. We were giving them words, but also giving them the power of using words to learn how to think biblically and express their opinions intelligently. We had our devotions with God, but it was also a time of family faith formation.

Over a period of several years, our informal approach to devotions began to develop into a pattern that we realized could be useful not just for family devotions, but also for other family times when we discussed the Scripture. Clay turned the pattern into what he called the "Family

Devotional ARTS," using a very simple acrostic for a devotional outline: **A**sk a question, **R**ead the Bible, **T**alk about it, and **S**peak to God. The ARTS outline became the heart of a family devotional and discipleship tool Clay then wrote called *Our 24 Family Ways*. It became a favorite resource for many of our own family devotions through the years, as well as for thousands of other families. The addendum for this book includes a similar resource called "Our 24 Family Words of Life," based on the principles of word-giving we've discussed. It also includes a fuller explanation about how to create an ARTS outline. We hope it will give you a start at creating a verbal atmosphere in your home where family faith formation can happen naturally and enjoyably.

Giving the Words You Believe

Before we talk about giving words that are believable and faith-forming to your children, we need to talk about the faith that is forming you, their parents. Remember, you cannot verbally pass on a faith to your children's hearts that is not settled in your own. Paul says, "We walk by faith, not by sight" (2 Corinthians 5:7)—our life as believers is defined by what we *cannot* see, not by what we *can* see. The author of Hebrews says the same—"Now faith is confidence in what we hope for and assurance about what we do not see"—and five verses later takes it one logical step further: "And without faith it is impossible to please God, because anyone who comes to him must believe that he exists and that he rewards those who earnestly seek him" (11:1, 6 NIV). Faith in an invisible, all-powerful, personal, and relational God is a nonnegotiable component of Christian parenting.

Without it, you can still be a good parent, but not a good *Christian* parent.

We cannot address all the biblical stories and truths that make claims on your faith as a Christian parent, and that will inform the words you give to form the faith of your children—from miracles to epiphanies to angels to heaven to demons to hell to prophecies to promises and many more. But we can mention four mega-truths of Christianity that you must, as a Christian parent, be able to claim confidently—incarnation, inspiration, transformation, and resurrection. Consider them a spiritual barometer to measure the confidence levels of your faith.

Incarnation

Without the incarnation, there is no "God with us" (Matthew 1:23), no "I and the Father are one" (John 10:30), no crucifixion, no atonement, no resurrection, no ascension. Without the incarnation, there is no Christianity. The apostle John said, "And the Word became flesh, and dwelt among us, and we saw His glory, glory as of the only begotten from the Father, full of grace and truth" (John 1:14). Jesus was the ultimate "thin place," an ancient Christian Celtic expression for places where heaven and earth meet. British theologian N. T. Wright says, "Part of the central achievement of the incarnation, which is celebrated in the resurrection and ascension, is that heaven and earth are now joined together with an unbreakable bond and that we too are by rights citizens of both together."[4] All the words you will give to your children as a Christian parent begin and end with your confident faith and belief in the incarnation of Jesus, who is Christ the Lord.

191

For John, the incarnation was a litmus test for anyone claiming divine spiritual authority: "This is how you can recognize the Spirit of God: Every spirit that acknowledges that Jesus Christ has come in the flesh is from God" (1 John 4:2 NIV). His statement reflects the words of Jesus, at His Last Supper, given to His disciples: "Do you not believe that I am in the Father, and the Father is in Me? The words that I say to you I do not speak on My own, but the Father, as He remains in Me, does His works" (John 14:10). It is a question that we, as Christian parents, must also answer as we seek to form faith in our children.

Inspiration

Without inspiration, the Bible we read as God's Word would be no more authoritative than any other religious holy book. But our Scripture claims to be more: "All Scripture is inspired by God" (2 Timothy 3:16). The Greek word for "inspired," *theopneustos*, literally means "God-breathed." The word *breathed* shares the same root as the word for Spirit, *pneuma*, so inspired, God-breathed Scripture is imbued with the Spirit of God. The author of Hebrews asserts that "the word of God is living and active and sharper than any two-edged sword, and piercing as far as the division of soul and spirit" (4:12). That human spirit is also *pneuma*, where the Holy Spirit does its work with the word of God. To give your children lifegiving words, enlivened by the Spirit of God, means giving them God-breathed Scripture.

That seems straightforward enough, but anyone who studies the history of how we got our Bible, and the varied views about translation and interpretation, knows that just as we accept the incarnation of Jesus by faith, we also must accept the inspiration of Scripture by faith. Like Jesus, the Bible is also a divine-human incarnation, the unfolding story of creation, fall, redemption, and restoration, told over a thousand years, by at least forty authors, in sixty-six books and letters, written in three ancient languages, and now translated into over seven hundred modern languages. Our Bible is not just a holy handbook about Christianity, but a divinely told story revealing the heart and purpose of our God for us, His creatures. Whatever questions you may have about Scripture, you can trust that the Holy Spirit of God is at work in and through the word of God that you give to your children. Your settled faith in the inspiration of Scripture will give your children confidence in the word and words of God.

Transformation

If incarnation is God becoming a human, and inspiration is God revealing himself to and through humans, then transformation is God living within humans. We are transformed not just to be trophies of divine beneficence, but to be objects of our Maker's longsuffering and faithful love. "For God so loved the world that he gave his one and only Son, that whoever believes in him shall not perish but have eternal life" (John 3:16 NIV). Through our human belief in the incarnated and resurrected Christ, revealed to us in God's inspired word, we can be transformed to live with Him forever. When you live out and talk about that transformation in your own life with your children, you are giving words of faith to them about sin, salvation, justification, forgiveness, sanctification, resurrection, glorification, and others. They will learn how to believe from what you believe.

193

Transformation is changing from one thing into another. In Greek, it is the word *metamorphoo*, literally to "change form." Jesus was transformed, or "transfigured," on the mountain with Peter, James, and John (see Matthew 17:2). But it is Paul who commands that we as believers must be transformed: "And do not be conformed to this world, but be transformed by the renewing of your mind, so that you may prove what the will of God is, that which is good and acceptable and perfect" (Romans 12:2). Paul also affirms the reality of that ongoing transforming change, that we "are being transformed into his image with ever-increasing glory, which comes from the Lord, who is the Spirit" (2 Corinthians 3:18 NIV). By the work of the Holy Spirit, we are becoming more and more like Christ, and in that process you are making personal transformation by the Spirit believable to your children. If it is believable to you, then it will also be to them.

Resurrection

Beyond (*meta*) the three mega-truths so far, resurrection is better considered a meta-truth that transcends and connects them all. *Resurrection engages incarnation.* God's eternal plan for the salvation of mankind included the life, death, and resurrection of Jesus. "Blessed be the God and Father of our Lord Jesus Christ, who according to His great mercy has caused us to be born again to a living hope through the resurrection of Jesus Christ from the dead" (1 Peter 1:3). *Resurrection engages inspiration.* Scripture is our only testimony to the resurrection of Christ. "That I may know Him and the power of His resurrection and the fellowship of His sufferings, being conformed to His death" (Philippians 3:10). *Resurrection engages transformation.* Our ultimate hope of transformation is that we too will be resurrected from the dead. "For if we have become united with Him in the likeness of His death, certainly we shall also be in the likeness of His resurrection" (Romans 6:5).

Paul clearly proclaims the centrality of the resurrection as a meta-truth for our faith: "But if there is no resurrection of the dead, not even Christ has been raised; and if Christ has not been raised, then our preaching is vain, your faith also is vain" (1 Corinthians 15:13–14). If the words you give to your children do not include that Jesus died and was resurrected from the dead, then the faith you are offering is a dead faith. It is the gospel, the good news of salvation, that we have been saved from death and delivered by faith into eternal life with Christ. There are no more important, believable words to give to your children than the Easter morning salutation "Christ is risen! He is risen indeed."

Forming Faith in the Family

Giving words that are believable does not happen best in formal lessons or lectures, but rather in the dailiness of real life in our home—at meals, sitting on couches, playing in the yard, working in the garage, at bedtimes. We found that faith grows best in the soil of real life, so there were always intentional times we planned into our life at home when we could sow seeds of truth into the "good soil" of our children's hearts. For the rest of this chapter, we want to suggest just a few of the intentional habits and patterns in our family that provided opportunities for believable words of faith to be given and discussed. We hope the four we share will encourage you to come up with more of your own.

Stories of Faith and Belief (Bible Stories of Faith)

Bible reading in our family grew in importance as the audience and ages grew. In these digital days of information fragmentation and saturation, Bible reading is being reduced to spiritual snippets. We knew we needed to include long readings in our family Bible reading habits, not just to make our children endure Mom and Dad making them listen, but to train their hearts and minds to hear and enter the bigger story that Scripture tells. Our friend Glenn Paauw, in his book *Saving the Bible from Ourselves*, says, "The biggest thing to do with the Bible is to read its overall story as *the Story*, and to do so with such regularity and in such depth that we can begin to reimagine our personal and community stories as part of its world-restoring drama."[5] Otherwise, in N. T. Wright's words, we read Scripture only as "rambling ways of declaring unstoried 'ideas.'"[6] Rather than fractional, functional, and informational snippets of Scripture, we wanted our children to hear real stories of real people who lived real lives of faith, and who believed in and lived for the God of Scripture. We wanted them to know about all of the Bible heroes in "God's Hall of Faith" in Hebrews chapter 11. We wanted the characters in the Bible's stories, and story, to be believable and to come alive and be alive for our children.

One way we did that was by reading both the Bible's stories and "story Bible" retellings of them. We believed in the spiritual power of Scripture to speak to our children's spirits, but also in the literary power of well-written retold narratives of those stories to speak to their imaginations—to bring to life the historical settings and characters with creativity, insight, and delightful storytelling. Rather than reading a commentary to *learn* those details, we would read stories to *live* them. We especially liked *The Child's Story Bible* (1935) by Catherine F. Vos for the literary quality of its stories. Just before we aged out with Bible story books, Sally Lloyd-Jones wrote *The Jesus Storybook Bible* (2007), an exceptionally well-written narrative of the Bible as one story about Jesus, the Savior. Even as teens, our boys enjoyed *The Action Bible* (2010), telling the stories with dramatic modern illustrations. If the Bible story book stays true to the Bible stories, it's an easy way to stimulate a time of verbal interaction that will cultivate and strengthen faith in your children and in you.

Testimonies of Faith and Belief (Believers' Stories of Faith)

Faith is not a subject that can be studied, learned, and mastered like language arts or arithmetic—knowledge about faith is not the same as personal belief. Christian parenting is walking with your child on the path of life and explaining along the way what it means to walk by faith. The goal of Christian parenting is to see your child believe the words of truth you give to them and then begin to walk on the path by faith on their own. In addition to *hearing* words that are believable, though, they also need to *see* those words lived out believably in the lives of others who walk or have walked by faith with Jesus. Yes, "faith comes from hearing, and hearing by the word of Christ" (Romans 10:17), but the author of Hebrews, after recalling the lives of countless Old Testament faithful followers of God who lived and died "by faith," also says that "since we have so great a cloud of witnesses surrounding us . . . let us run with endurance the race that is set before us" (12:1). Faith going forward is built on the faith of those who have come before us—their lives are a witness to believable faith.

Your children need to see in you, and in others living for Christ in this world, what John declared: "For whoever has been born of God overcomes the world; and this is the victory that has overcome the world: our faith" (1 John 5:4). Those testimonies of faith happen first in the body of Christ, the church. Even our children can learn from fellowship with other believers that walking with Jesus is a lifelong journey of faith. That is why we also made reading aloud the stories of faithful Christians a priority in our home. We focused on books because reading aloud, in contrast to passive media such as video, is an actively verbal experience—a way of giving your words. Reading engaged our children in a verbal interaction with us that also allowed for questions, observations, and other discourse. It was a powerful way to talk about the believability of faith in the lives of men and women of faith.

There are, of course, thousands of books about many kinds of faithful witnesses—missionaries, martyrs, leaders, pastors, and just ordinary people. We encourage you to find biographies and histories that are told creatively and well as stories, not just as factual accounts. Here are just a few suggestions from the many books that influenced our children:

- *Hero Tales*, 4 volumes: Fifteen Christian heroes (short bio, three anecdotal stories)
- CHRISTIAN HEROES: THEN & NOW series (YWAM): Fifty biographies of heroes of faith
- *God's Smuggler*: The story of Brother Andrew

- *Shadow of the Almighty*: The story of Jim Elliot
- *L'Abri*: The story of Francis and Edith Schaeffer
- *A Chance to Die*: The story of Amy Carmichael
- *The Hiding Place*: The story of Corrie ten Boom
- *A Passion for the Impossible*: The story of Lilias Trotter

Words of Faith and Belief (Bible Truths of Faith)

Every major scripture that deals directly with bringing up children touches on the idea of instruction at some level. For most, *instruction* elicits mental images of classrooms, teachers, workbooks, and tests. Historically, the church institutionalized the schooling model, with age-graded Sunday school, children's church, and Christian education departments. When we chose to homeschool our children, we quickly discarded the formal schooling model of learning and created our own home-centered approach to instruction. We believed God designed home as the primary living and learning environment for children, and we advocated a real-life, highly verbal, relational approach to learning modeled after how Jesus taught His disciples.

Our informal credo about God's word asserted that it is possible to learn the word without loving it, but it is impossible to love the word without learning it. We wanted our children to learn to love the word of God. So, like the disciples, they never completed a Bible curriculum, sat through lectures about Bible books, or took tests about their Bible knowledge. Instead, we gave believable words of truth to our children personally through verbal interaction with them about the Bible in the midst of real life. While we were all learning to live, we were also living to learn. (For more about our views on learning, see *Awaking Wonder* and *Educating the WholeHearted Child*, 4th edition.)

With so much more Christian "instruction" available now online, by video, and in print, in addition to the many high-energy and well-funded programs most churches offer for children, the temptation is even stronger for "modern" Christian parents to simply follow that easy road. It's possible now to avoid nearly all of the instructional work that God intended for parents to do with their children, but we encourage you to persevere in cultivating your life together at home to instruct your children. Be intentional about providing more informal times when you can give your children believable words of faith and belief.

If home has become little more than a way station between the activities of a too-busy life, it's time to consider how to simplify your lives to gain more time together as a family—at meals, on family nights, at bedtime, in the car. As you find those times, begin to think intentionally about using them to talk casually and informally about biblical truths you want your children to know. The point is not to lecture them, but to instruct them through verbal interaction and conversation, asking what they think and affirming their insights. Paul reminded Timothy that the words he had to give to others would be good because he had been "constantly nourished on the words of the faith and of the sound doctrine which you have been following" (1 Timothy 4:6), which is the goal of giving your words.

Acts of Faith and Belief (Our Stories of Faith)

When it comes to giving believable words to your children, there are few more personal words than your own stories of personal faith and belief. But beyond those, your children also need to hear about your *family's* stories of faith—how God has worked and is working through your faith by answering prayers, intervening to help, providing for needs, healing health problems, giving divine guidance. Those micro stories help them imagine a personal God who is involved in the spiritual life of your family.

But your children also need to hear words that are believable from a macro perspective, how your family fits into the overarching story that God is writing, that they have been chosen, redeemed, and sealed "in Christ" (see Ephesians 1:3–14), empowered and spiritually equipped by God himself to play a key part in His unfolding story of life and eternal life in the kingdom of heaven. They are the "whoever" John had in mind when he wrote, "For whoever has been born of God overcomes the world; and this is the victory that has overcome the world: our faith" (1 John 5:4). The world is a big and scary place, but you can remind your children that they can overcome fear with their faith.

In his last letter before his death, Paul wrote to his son in the faith, Timothy: "Retain the standard of sound words which you have heard from me, in the faith and love which are in Christ Jesus. Guard, through the Holy Spirit who dwells in us, the treasure which has been entrusted to you" (2 Timothy 1:13). You can lift the lid on that treasure entrusted by faith to Timothy by reading Paul's epistles to the Ephesians and the Colossians. All those "sound words" are the same words that you can give to your children with the Holy Spirit's help as part of your mission as a family in the world. In order to give your children sound words and treasured truth, believable words about your family's stories of faith and how your family is part of God's unfolding story in the world, you will need to fill the well of your spirit with His truth—read and study the Bible, read books that help you tell the story of faith in your family, talk with other godly men and women about faith, listen to trusted pastors and teachers. If the treasure is in your heart, then the Holy Spirit will give you believable words to give to your children, and they will use those words and take on the world for Christ: "In the world you have tribulation, but take courage; I have overcome the world" (John 16:33).

— • —

This final chapter in the "Giving Words" section has been much more about you, the parents, than about your children. That is necessary for the simple reason that *Giving Your Words* is as much about authenticity as it is about pragmatics. No matter how many practical ideas and suggestions we include in the book, if the words you give because of them are not coming from a place of spiritual authenticity in your own life, then your children will not find them believable for their developing faith. It's not that you will fail to *create* their faith, but rather that you can falter in *forming and cultivating* it. Henry Clay Trumbull (1830–1903) was a prolific Christian author, an evangelist, and a pioneer in the American Sunday school movement. He was also the father of eight grown children, all walking with the Lord, when he wrote *Hints on Child-Training* in 1890, a commonsense book about biblical principles for raising Christian children. Here's what he said about a child's faith: "There is no need of trying to implant faith in a child's nature, for it is there to begin with. But there is need of training a child's faith, so that it shall be rightly directed and wisely developed. Every child has the instinct of faith, as surely as it has the instinct of appetite."[7]

In order to rightly direct and wisely develop your child's emerging faith, the words you give to them must come from a settled yet always-seeking faith in your own heart. None of us ever reaches a spiritual plateau where we have somehow scaled the hill of faith and need go no farther. Paul admonishes us all, "Therefore if you have been raised up with Christ, *keep seeking* the things above, where Christ is, seated at the right hand of God. *Set your mind* on the things above, not on the things that are on earth. For you have died and your life is hidden with Christ in God" (Colossians 3:1–3, italics added). An authentic faith is not measured by how much you know about Scripture or the Christian life, but by how much you don't yet know but seek to learn. We'll close this chapter with Paul's encouragement: "So then, brothers and sisters, stand firm and hold fast to the teachings we passed on to you, whether by word of mouth or by letter" (2 Thessalonians 2:15 NIV). Stand firm and give your children faith-forming words that are believable.

Parenting
VERBALOGISTICS

South African pastor and author Andrew Murray (1828–1917) wisely said, "The confidence that our children will grow up true believers—something higher than the confidence they will eventually be saved—will exercise its influence on us and them. For us it is a daily call to a life of holiness and consecration; to our children it is an expectation of God's working in their lives to make them all He wants them to be."[8] One effective way to fulfill that expectation of God's work in your family is to give words to your children that are believable because they come from your own life with God. Exercise faith for both yourselves and your children by declaring a "Forty Days of Faith" family journey. Explain that every day during the journey you will ask and discuss one question: "How did we believe in God today as a family and put our trust in Him?" The answer may be little or large; the point is only to look and see "God with us." Whether on computer or on paper, keep a journey journal to record every day's answer. Choose a verse about faith for every day, or one for each week, or for every five days (there are over five hundred faith and belief verses in the New Testament). Make the words of Gabriel to Mary the theme verse for your journey: "For nothing will be impossible with God" (Luke 1:37).

Lifegiving
WORDS

TEN

Giving Words
That Give Life

*The Spirit is the one who gives life; human nature is
of no help! The words that I have spoken to you are
spirit and are life.*

John 6:63 NET

One of the Clarkson family traditions that was a unique
and intensive time of parental word-giving was our family high school graduation celebration. As homeschoolers,
each of our children took part in a formal graduation with
others in their umbrella school or support group, but our
home celebration was just for our family and a few select
friends. It was always a special day, with invitations sent out
early to make sure the date was secure for family friends we
wanted there to share in our child's big day. We decorated
with graduation accoutrements, put out favorite homemade

foods and baked goodies, mixed up sweet refreshments, lit candles, put on music to greet the guests, and dressed up at least a little (gown and mortarboard not required). It was a celebration to be sure, but also a serious commencement ceremony with the bestowing of a diploma, so we tried to strike the right balance for the occasion.

Though festive, our family graduation party was more than just a social event. It was a time to celebrate the life of the graduating child and charge them to seek God's direction and call on their life as a Christian and as a woman or man of God. From the first one with Sarah in 2000 to the last one with Joy in 2011, each celebration retained the same elements: singing hymns and spiritual songs to begin, including a song written by Clay for that graduating child; presentation of their graduation diploma and a framed manuscripture (a limited edition calligraphy) of Proverbs 3:5–6; a parentally required valedictory address; ten specially chosen commencement gifts, each with a related charge or encouragement delivered by one of us; sharing wisdom and praying for the graduate; singing "Step by Step" by Rich Mullins as a closing song; and ending with a benediction. A printed bulletin memorialized the event for each child and for all who attended.

The heart of the ceremony was giving the ten gifts and gift-related words with personalized parental charges based on one or more selected scriptures. Several of the gifts were repeated for each child: a framed family portrait ("Remember your heritage of faith and family"), a leather-bound study Bible ("Seek the God of truth and the truth of God in His word"), a cross ("Live for Christ and His gospel every day"), an oil lamp or candle ("Let your light shine for all to see"), a journal ("Use your life and gifts to honor God"), and of course a selection of good books ("Grow in maturity as a whole person"). But other symbolic gifts were personalized for each child. Sarah received writing paper with a charge to be a steward of her writing gifts, and a teacup and cozy to symbolize Christian hospitality. Joel received a pottery basin and towel with a charge to serve others with love and humility, and an eagle plaque to remind him to persevere with God. Nathan received a *Jesus* DVD to remind him to serve others, and a special copy of *The Message* to seek God's guidance daily. Joy received a keychain symbolizing being a woman after God's heart, and a plaque to remind her to persevere in serving others with patience and humility.

Proverbs 3:5–6 was the theme verse for every graduation: "Trust in the LORD with all your heart and do not lean on your own understanding. In all your ways acknowledge Him, and He will make your paths straight." You can see why those verses are "graduation" words, especially if you read verses 1–4 just before them: "My son, do not forget my teaching, but let your heart keep my commandments. . . . Do not let kindness and truth leave you. . . . So you will find favor and good repute in the sight of God and man." Solomon was admonishing his teenage son to prepare him to graduate from being a young man to becoming an adult. Verses 5–6, then, are his personal charge of godly wisdom to his child. He was giving words to his son, just as we would follow his example and give words to our children—sending them from our home into the world with words of personal counsel, godly wisdom, vision, and love. For us, each graduation celebration was the ninety-minute ultimate expression of our parental role as word givers, and the "Giving Our Words" equivalent of a State of the Union message—we were planting a flag of faith, hope, and love in our children's hearts with our words. And then, of course, it became a fun family social event—a great potluck meal or dessert buffet, and lots of time for fellowship with friends. All things in balance.

Graduating to a Verbal Home

Perhaps graduation is a useful metaphor for the purpose of this book. We want to encourage Christian parents to consider graduating not *from* something, but *to* a new way of looking at their home and family life. In modern terms, we want to encourage you to graduate from a virtual home to a verbal home. In a virtual home, most of the words about Christian faith are given virtually, through secondary sources and media such as TV, video, audio, and print. There's nothing wrong with those sources per se, except when they supplant or even replace the role of real verbal interaction at home. We encourage you to consider graduating to becoming a truly verbal home, where most of the words about faith are given verbally, from one person's heart (yours) to another's (your child's).

That fundamental move from virtual to verbal would make the biggest change in the spirit of your home. However, it would also provide for other graduations of change. For instance, you could move from an informational model of Christian home building to a formational model. An informational model is about what your children know—your child's knowledge about the Bible, which is a good thing, wrongly becomes the barometer of successful Christian parenting. A formational model is about what your children are becoming—your child's walk and relationship with God is the focus of your relationship with them. In faith formation, you are following biblical patterns of discipleship—modeling, mentoring, instructing, training—in order to be the primary spiritual influence in your child's life. And that leads naturally into defining what a Christian home really is. We mentioned it earlier in the book, but it needs to be repeated: A Christian home can never be defined only by what your children are doing; it is defined and determined by what you, their parents, are doing. Perhaps graduating from a virtual home to a verbal home will be your first step toward building a truly Christian home.

The most powerful tool parents have to shape their children's lives is their words—lifegiving words of truth that will tell each child who they are, and will form the person they are becoming. When they "take your words for it," they will be changed by them. Giving your words is about being a witness to the truth of Scripture for your children and living with them as a model of the faith you want them to adopt. It's about being nurturing parents who engage verbally with their children to "bring them up in the discipline and instruction of the Lord." It's about imitating the example of Paul, who described himself with the most familial words possible—as a nursing *mother* who tenderly and lovingly cares for her children with words of hope, and as a caring and involved *father* who implores his children to live for God and His kingdom (see 1 Thessalonians 2:7–12). Giving your words is a family matter!

In his letter to the Colossian church, Paul provides the key to modeling the faith you want your children to adopt: "Let the message about Christ, in all its richness, fill your lives.

Teach and counsel each other with all the wisdom he gives" (3:16 NLT). It's not complicated. Stay filled up with the Spirit of Christ and share what you're learning from Him with your children. That's it. There is no program, video, or workbook that will model faith for you. It's just you. Paul wraps up that thought with "And whatever you do or say, do it as a representative of the Lord Jesus, giving thanks through him to God the Father" (v. 17 NLT). That may sound more spiritual than you feel you can be, but it's just walking with Christ by faith every day, reading the Bible, praying, and talking to your kids about your relationship with the Lord and what you're learning in Scripture. If you're doing that, then you're already on your way to a *Giving Your Words* kind of life.

Daniel: A Graduation Story

There is one more graduation story we want to share. It is the untold story of "Daniel in the Parents' Den." Yes, that Daniel. This story is not told in Scripture, yet it is not difficult to imagine that it might have happened. All we know about Daniel, one of the four major prophets of Israel, is from the book that bears his name. We first meet him as a young man, probably an adolescent of about sixteen, freshly exiled from Jerusalem to Babylon in 605 BC. King Nebuchadnezzar orders his officials to educate Daniel and other Hebrew youths for three years in the Babylonian literature and language to prepare them for service in his courts. They are described as "young men without any physical defect, handsome, showing aptitude for every kind of learning, well informed, quick to understand, and qualified to serve in the king's palace" (Daniel 1:4 NIV). The book of Daniel tells their story.

The story we want to tell, though, is what might have happened in the years leading up to that scene. For that, we need to go back to Jerusalem. After Assyria conquered and scattered the ten northern tribes of Israel in 722 BC, the two remaining tribes of Judah in the south suffered under a string of mostly bad kings who forsook God. In 640 BC, though, Josiah becomes king of Judah at eight years old; at sixteen he begins to seek God; at twenty he cleanses the land of pagan altars and idols; and in 622 BC, at age twenty-six, while restoring the temple, he discovers the forgotten "book of the law of the LORD given by Moses" (2 Chronicles 34:14). He is deeply convicted to walk after the Lord and to keep the Law with all his heart and soul, and a revival begins in Judah. It will be short-lived, though, as the good and godly king Josiah tragically dies in battle at age thirty-nine (for Josiah's story, see 2 Chronicles 34–35).

But what if a young couple in Josiah's courts were also deeply convicted when the revival began, gave their lives to the Lord, and had a son? What if they brought up their son in the ways of God's Law, but when the boy was about twelve years old, Josiah died? What if that mother and father, knowing that the time would be short for Jerusalem, began to prepare their son for an uncertain future by instructing him in all the ways and wisdom of God? They would love him fiercely, giving him all the words of faith and truth they could. Four years later, when their son was sixteen, the same age at which Josiah turned to God, Nebuchadnezzar laid siege to Jerusalem and took the best and brightest of Judah's youth back to Babylon. Another captivity in 597 BC and the final destruction of Jerusalem and the temple in 586 BC are yet to come, but the young man by then will be a leader in the courts of the Babylonian king, preparing to be a voice for God and His people. The boy's name, of course, is Daniel.

Daniel can be a helpful story of graduation for Christian parents living in uncertain times. Though we know nothing about Daniel's parents, we do know that he was prepared as a young teen, recognized for his intellect, wisdom, social skills, and even spirituality, and was ready to follow God even in Babylon. In our family, we imagined that he had been prepared by godly parents who considered the times in which they were living and did all they could to ready their son to live for God. That parental preparation would surely have been verbal. Perhaps they too would have given Daniel a papyrus of the proverb we gave to all our children for graduation, reminding him to trust the Lord wholeheartedly—"In all your ways acknowledge Him, and He will make your paths straight" (3:6). Daniel's graduation was unexpected and severe, yet he was ready for the path ahead. In these uncertain times, perhaps this imagined story can be an encouragement to seriously consider becoming a more verbal parent to prepare your children for their own journeys of faith with God.

The Good Way of God

At this point in our lives, we can honestly say we've felt a bit of what Daniel's imagined parents might have felt. We've graduated four children into the world, and though none of them has been exiled by a hostile king to a foreign country, they have all gone far and wide from our home. We raised them to listen to God, set their sights high, and follow the Lord wherever He might lead them, so the resulting paths have been quite varied. But perhaps our progeny are just taking after their parents, since we lived much the same way in our own days of youth and even after marriage. While our children were in our home, though, we are confident that our words prepared them to live by faith and make godly choices when we graduated them into their lives as adults.

Around the same time that the stories of Josiah and Daniel were unfolding, Jeremiah was prophesying to Judah about Babylon. Even as the shadow was coming over them, he reminded the people, "This is what the LORD says: 'Stand at the crossroads and look; ask for the ancient paths, ask where the good way is, and walk in it, and you will find rest for your souls'" (6:16 NIV). Now it feels like there are numerous crossroads moments in our lives—times when we and our children are faced with choices about the paths ahead of us. Whatever the crossroads may be, the wisdom still applies: "Ask where the good way is, and walk in it." It all comes back to the same trusted words and ways of God that we have taught and talked about with our children for thirty-something years. Those words are not just child-friendly truth-bites that we would serve up along the way when it was convenient and useful. They are the words we have always given to our children, the same truths that have shaped each of our lives as their parents for over fifty years as we have walked with God on the path of life.

We are still asking where that "good way" is so we can walk in it as we continue to give our words to our now adult children. Even as we are farther along the path, we still are yearning for the way and learning how to see it better. As Solomon explains to his sons, "But the path of the righteous is like the light of dawn, that shines brighter and brighter until the full day" (Proverbs 4:18). He wanted his children to understand that the farther you walk with God on His path of life, the more you will see, the more you will have to say about walking with God, and the more of His light you will find. We know now that light is found in Jesus as we walk with Him, who is the "Light of the world" and the "Light of life" for us (John 8:12).

We want the words we give to our children to be lifegiving words of the Spirit, the kind that Jesus gave. In *The Peshitta Holy Bible*, from the language that Jesus spoke, He is called "The Lifegiver of the world" (John 4:42). Jesus told His disciples, "It is the Spirit who gives life . . . the words that I have spoken to you are spirit and are life" (John 6:63). When you give your words from the life of the Spirit living within you, you are giving your children lifegiving words. We echo the words of Peter: "Lord, to whom shall we go? You have words of eternal life" (v. 68).

We pray that God's light—His truth and wisdom—will shine brighter every day as you walk with Him on the path of life, the good way of God. And we pray that the light and life of Christ will shine brightly in the words you give to your children as they walk with you. As we come to the end of this journey of giving your words, we'll recall where we started, with God's words expressing what we hope for the words we give as parents: "So is my word that goes out from my mouth: It will not return to me empty, but will accomplish what I desire and achieve the purpose for which I sent it" (Isaiah 55:11 NIV). May your words give the light and life of Christ to your children as you lead them to the good way of God.

Epilogue

THE WORDS OF THEIR LIVES

Children are a heritage from the Lord, *offspring a reward from him.*

Psalm 127:3 NIV

We opened this book with the "Words of *Our* Lives" and then told the stories of how we gave our words to our children. But we want to end with the "Words of *Their* Lives" so you can hear from our children themselves. Since they are both the subjects of the book and the objects of our word-giving, it seemed fitting to give our children the last words. They are all grown now—Sarah a mother, author, podcaster, teacher; Joel a doctoral student, author, composer, musician; Nathan a filmmaker, actor, author, podcaster; Joy a doctoral graduate, author, podcaster, editor. We simply asked each of our wonderful children how they remember our words and the verbal atmosphere of our home during their growing-up years, and if there might be a word story that stands out in their memory.

It also seems fitting to close with a scripture that catches the spirit of family and word-giving. However, out of the 782,815 words in our NASB translation of choice, there are surprisingly few about children. So please forgive us for using a verse here out of context. John is actually talking about his child in faith, Gaius, a leader in the church, but his words ring true for anyone with children. So we'll join the long history of Christian parents who misappropriate this verse with good intentions. It certainly expresses what we feel about our own children: "I have no greater joy than this, to hear of my children walking in the truth" (3 John 1:4). Here are our children, who are indeed our greatest joy, walking in the truth.

Sarah Clarkson

Words were wielded in my childhood home with a kind of creative enchantment, used in the very way that God himself uses them throughout Scripture: to call things into being, to name, to order, and to bless. Our souls and bodies are spoken alive by the living Word, and the bright, kindled words we speak have the power to call goodness, truth, and beauty into being all around us. Parents have the power to set their children in a certain kind of life, a certain quality of existence, by the very words they use each day. Every word we hear in small childhood teaches us what things are important, what people are for, what beauty means, what kindness sounds like, what love can create when it is spoken.

One gift of words my parents offered stands out to me particularly in the long halls of memory, and that was the yearly offering of birthday praise. It was simple in practice—after the opening of presents and the eating of the birthday breakfast cinnamon rolls, each person in the family had to say one good or kind thing about the birthday child. It could be admiration for a talent, recognition of growth or skill, thanks for a certain service or attention, or just the expression of affection. Nothing was prescribed except kindness, and there was certainly no backing out of this obligation.

Introvert that I am, I remember feeling shy every birthday as the time came for the words to be spoken. But I would not have skipped those moments for the world. For splendid as the presents might be, it was the gift of praise from those who knew me best, for good and ill, that set me in a kind of startled sense of blessing each year.

My parents' words were always of affirmation. Each would often name ways in which I had developed and flourished, honoring my new capacities in writing or music, my patience with siblings, or grit in a hard task. Their praise gave form and substance, in the way almost of an epic poem, to all the ways I was growing, and all the distinct and individual ways they loved me, not just as one of the kids, but as Sarah—watched, cultivated, beloved.

But it was the words of my siblings that often startled me. These all-too-mortal, ordinary beings with whom, as C. S. Lewis said, we "joke with, work with, marry, snub, and exploit"[1] (well, no marriage in this case), would suddenly say something of such blazing kindness or insight that I felt myself knocked off my mental feet and set up for life all in a moment. One brother praised my wisdom in a year when I often felt myself incapable of making myself heard: "I wait to hear what you'll say," he said. "I've seen your courage," said my sister in another year, a hidden year, when victories were the tiny ones of hope on any given day. "I love the way you weave words," said the brother whose own words and music were a glory.

This birthday gift of words is one I will teach my own children to offer, because for me those were potent words of love and empowerment, of tender recognition, and of belonging. By asking us to articulate what we loved about each other, my parents taught us the language of affection, quickening in us the capacity to praise the beauty in another and to create communion by offering affection. Those birthday words influenced the whole of the way we learned to speak to each other as siblings; their beauty shaped the whole of our story as a family. Such words will, I hope, shape my children's story as well.

Joel Clarkson

There was always silence in the beginning. Often, it was, at first, a restless quietude, not entirely sanctified, of fidgeting and sniffling and coughing. The echoes of laughter and conversation reverberating in our minds often took time to fade as we turned our attention to the artistry at hand. Eventually, though, into this moment of familial liturgy, a subliminal awareness, hidden for much of the day, would rise to the surface.

The blank canvas of our family prayer time awaited the first stroke.

Often, it was a parent who took the first swipe of the brush. Their lines were invariably strong and straight, words of praise that outlined the shape of our gratitude to God and our petition for His help in our daily needs. Soon, they would draw the brush full circle to where they began in praise, and would step back from the art. Now it was our turn.

One of my younger siblings began their own offering, dotting the art with pointillistic words typical of youthful prayerfulness. Bright pastels of simple requests and innocent reflections acted as a gentle contrast to the strength and clarity of our parents' intercession. With each sibling's added prayer, new hues, textures, and patterns emerged, words particular to each personality and view of the world. In this improvisatory offering, each child was invited to imagine our own creative capacity to come into relationship, through our words, with the Creator and Redeemer of the universe, revealed as the Word made flesh. Our family prayer initiated us into the great, unending act of praise that the angels themselves eternally offer, to set our own intercessions and thanksgivings as an act of worshipful artistry in continuity with the masterstrokes of the Divine.

Soon, all others had made their offering, and my turn at the easel had come. The work before me had already come gloriously into being. What could I add to it? I let the stillness center within me once more and listened for the voice inside me, the Word, the *logos*, which my parents had always shown me was there, to help me speak. Out of that Word, Christ within me, I set my own words to blank space before me.

As an introvert, embodying an artistic temperament from early childhood, my expression took on shades of a subtler sort; my words of reflection brought forth impressionistic indigos and sea-grays. Gradually, as my confidence grew, the color of my words shifted to warmer tones of crimson edged almost imperceptibly with gold, and my petitions returned to the visual center of the art—the swirling, radiant, poly-chromatic dance of praise. Soon, I let the brush of my words slide lightly from the surface and stood back, my offering integrated into the whole.

Soon, the prayer would be concluded, the art removed from the easel, and as a family, we would raise up our work of words, created in and through Christ, back to the Father, in the power of the Holy Spirit. In that moment, I knew I had been given the agency to partake, as a willing and able member, in the great work to which all prayer contributes until the end of time—the never-ceasing doxology offered as a gift, received from the author of light, and given back to Him in gratitude. Even now, each day, I reflect in gratitude upon the opportunity to reenter that creativity of spoken-ness, once again lifting up my heart in my own words of thanks and praise, to the master artist who makes all prayer into a masterpiece in himself.

Nathan Clarkson

My palms were sweating and heart racing, pumping anger, embarrassment, and shame into every inch of my thirteen-year-old adolescent body. Every eye in the classroom was on me as I sat in the hard plastic classroom chair looking up into the livid eyes of a teacher's aide who'd finally had enough. I hadn't *tried* to be "bad," but in the exuberance of being a newly minted teen boy attempting to make his friends laugh, mixed with a genuine curiosity that kept me asking questions my teacher couldn't (or didn't want to) answer, I found myself on the wrong side of a tired teacher's ire. After the initial sur-prise of being in trouble, I was physically grabbed, dragged outside the classroom, and scolded. In the flush of emotion, the words sounded to me like adults in a Charlie Brown cartoon, only angrier, and they cut deeply into my heart. I wanted to fight back, to explain why the teacher was wrong about me. But the words that usually came easily failed me, and all that came were tears. The pent-up frustration of being misunderstood began to seep out from the corners of my eyes. Embarrassed at my emotional reaction, I looked at the floor as I was escorted to a private area to wait for my mom to pick me up. Dread crept over my young heart at the thought of having to explain to her, yet again, how my unruly nature had gotten me in trouble. But instead of the disappointment I anticipated, I was met with love. Back home, after I explained what happened, my mom began the work of undoing the destructive words cast over me by my teacher. With lifegiving words, she spoke into my wounded spirit, affirming my exuberance, wit, curiosity, sense of humor, and mind. They were not mistakes, but good and beautiful qualities in me that God could use in a special way in the story He had for me to tell.

Early in my life I knew I was different. I could see other kids, even my siblings, who seemed to move about the world in a way I simply could not. Eventually, I was diagnosed with severe OCD, ADHD, ODD, dyslexia, and later depression. Those letters and words of "disorders" felt like a life sentence, separating me from the world and holding me back from the dreams, relationships, and life I so deeply desired. Every time I found myself in trouble with yet another angry instructor, it just underlined the reality of their hurtful words about me. And each time, I was tempted to believe lies about myself—that I was too different, too much, and just too inherently messed up. But my mom was always there as an advocate—fighting fire with fire, words with words, contesting every negative, demeaning, and hurtful word about me, whether from others or myself. With her true, encouraging, hopeful, and empowering words, she reminded me who I really was.

Words have been powerful in my life, in both dark and beautiful ways, shaping how I see reality, God, and even myself. Wisely, though, no matter what damaging or demeaning words attacked my spirit, my parents understood the power of those words too, and they would be there with words of life to shine light into my darkness. As a grown man now, those old negative words spoken of me still hurt, but words of beauty spoken over me, all these years later, continue to give me strength to keep going, to believe the truth about myself, and to live the story I was created to tell.

Joy Clarkson

"What story will you tell with your life?"

This question was an ongoing topic of conversation throughout my young adulthood. During my teen years, my mom would take me out to coffee on Saturday mornings. We walked downtown along old streets lined with beautiful houses, we sipped coffee, we talked about everything under heaven. Our conversations often drifted toward aspirations: What did I want to do with my life? What did I love, care about, find myself drawn to? How might my passions and the world's needs meet? How might God use me?

During my senior year of college, I decided that I wanted to pursue a master's degree in theology, to research, teach, and write. A week after I had gotten into a dream program, I traveled back to Colorado for a debate tournament and met my dad for breakfast. After I ordered an omelet and breakfast potatoes, and he ordered oatmeal with blueberries, my dad produced an impressive and mysterious binder. I opened it and flipped through the pages. There I found biographies of all the professors at the university and descriptions of classes I was likely to take.

"I'm really excited for you," he said, "and I thought it might be fun to talk about what you hope to learn in this program."

In my mother's ongoing and intentional exploration of my hopes and dreams, and my father's thoughtful binder and good questions, I see one of the most influential ways my parents gave me and my siblings their words: by helping us discover and articulate a vision for living a meaningful life. They did this in three ways.

First, they verbalized the strengths and passions they saw emerging in our young lives. My parents were students of me and my siblings, watching for signs of giftedness, listening to the passions of our hearts. It is one thing to love writing or be good at science, and another to have someone say, "You are really gifted with words" or "I think you would make an amazing scientist." There is a profound power in saying the good things you see in someone else's life out loud. My parents were intentional to call out the good they saw in us and encourage us to grow.

Second, they engaged us in conversation, helping us dream about how we might live purposefully and put our skills to good use for God's kingdom. The root of the word *question* is *quest*, and many of the paths I've chosen to take in life began with a "quest-ion" that my parents helped draw out. Through conversation, discoveries were made and convictions were deepened. What do you love doing? Who do you want to become? How might God use your gifts and talents to influence the world and help others? What kind of life do you want to have? These questions were part of an ongoing conversation, infinitely interesting to my parents, about who we would become. And in engaging us in that discussion, the path ahead began to unfold.

Finally, they spoke forward into our lives, expecting goodness and beauty. Even when we were in difficult, awkward, or rebellious stages, my mother was unwaveringly positive in her language about our future lives: "I know this is hard, but I believe you are going to be so strong and loving." There was a sense of unfolding, blossoming, a story reaching a new and beautiful fullness that was always, somehow, expected. Hearing my parents verbally anticipate a good, godly, and meaningful life for me gave me the strength to press on, stay faithful, and have hope. They gave me words of life, and words to live by.

Our 24 Family Words of Life

Values and truths that you want to give to your children are not just objective, impersonal statements to be memorized and recited. You can fill your children's minds with words, but those words will not shape their lives and choices until they fill and shape their hearts and souls. Words become ways that influence a child's walk with God only when they work into that child's inner being.

Early in our ministry we created a tool for parenting called *Our 24 Family Ways*. It is a discipleship resource for teaching biblical family values in a way that can reach your children's hearts and souls. Its verbal and relational approach helps children internalize and remember the biblical family values we wanted to give them.

The devotional outlines below use the same "Family Devotional ARTS" model we created for *Our 24 Family Ways*, but this resource is much shorter. Still, it is enough to give you an example of how to create your own "Words of Life" to give to your children. We encourage you to do a concordance study of each "word" so you can add four to five additional devotions. Or do your own topical studies to identify new word categories and biblical words to build your own "Words of Life" ARTS devotions to give to your children. The ARTS outline is a tool to help you build a verbal home. Use it for any Bible content. Here's how it works.

A **Ask a Question**—The purpose of the opening question is to gain the interest and attention of your children. It should be an open-ended question that generates conversation and elicits an opinion or insight, not just a "right answer." Typically, it is not directly about the Bible passage, but rather will lead naturally into it.

R **Read the Bible**—Once everyone is engaged and listening, read aloud the Bible passage. Here is where the "Saying the Words" skills enter into the ARTS model. Read the Scripture in a way that will be heard—with dramatic expression, timing, pacing, and emphasis. Show with your voice that you believe God's word is alive with truth.

T **Talk about It**—Here the devotional moves into the personal, relational, interactional phase. Ask questions that will help your children do more than just repeat the Bible content you've read, but rather find examples, principles, and life applications in the passage. Help them to not merely listen for the words, but to discern God's voice.

S **Speak to God**—The final step is not the typical and often-tacked-on "do this today" application. Rather, it is about what should always be the first and most important application after reading any Bible passage: prayer. With this step, you are teaching your children how to respond to God in prayer, and how to pray.

The words and "ways" that follow are first-step examples of one way to cultivate the verbal habit and practice in your family of talking, conversing, and interacting about God's word. The ways are grouped into six topical categories: Truth, Grace, Faith, Hope, Love, and Life. Each of the six topics includes a scripture that can be used as a memory verse, and then four ways about the topic, each with a full ARTS outline. The ways are not set in stone, so feel free to restate any of them for your own family. Even better, come up with new ways that are all your own. You will give your children words that will shape their hearts and minds for the rest of their lives, and also train them in relational and verbal skills for telling others about God and His word.

Giving Words of TRUTH

John 1:14—And the Word became flesh, and dwelt among us, and we saw His glory, glory as of the only begotten from the Father, full of grace and truth.

Word #1—Word

In our family, we read and trust God's word, the Bible, because in it we find God's truth and wisdom for life.

ASK: If someone writes a book about you but the title can have only one word (not your name), what would you want it to be?

READ: Hebrews 4:12—For the word of God is living and active and sharper than any two-edged sword, and piercing as far as the division of soul and spirit, of both joints and marrow, and able to judge the thoughts and intentions of the heart.

TALK: The word of God is God's revealed truth, not just the Bible. How is it a spiritual sword, and how does it pierce a "soul and spirit"? What does the writer say that the sharpness of the word of God in a spiritual heart does?

SPEAK: Thank God for His word that speaks to your heart. Ask Him to pierce your heart with His sword of truth to sharpen your own character and trust in Him.

Word #2—Wisdom

In our family, we seek true wisdom from God's word that enables us to walk by faith every day with Him.

ASK: What was the wisest thing you said or did this week?

READ: Ephesians 5:15–16—Therefore be careful how you walk, not as unwise men but as wise, making the most of your time, because the days are evil.

TALK: Walk is another word in Scripture for how you live. What does Paul mean about being careful to walk wisely? How do we make the most of time wisely (literally, redeem the time)? How does wisdom help us be careful about evil?

SPEAK: Pray that you will seek the wisdom of God to live a wise life with Him. Ask for wisdom so you can make the most of the days God gives to you.

Word #3—Instruction

In our family, we study and learn God's word so we can know Him personally and know how to live for Him faithfully.

Ask: What is something you do well that you could teach a friend to do?

Read: 2 Timothy 3:16–17—All Scripture is inspired by God and profitable for teaching, for reproof, for correction, for training in righteousness; so that the man of God may be adequate, equipped for every good work.

Talk: The New International Version says that all Scripture is "God-breathed." How does that help you understand what *inspired* means in other Bible versions? What four ways does Paul say that Scripture equips us to be God's workers? How do you experience each one?

Speak: Thank God that He has revealed himself to you in the Bible so you can know Him and His truth. Ask Him to use Scripture to equip you for His work.

Word #4—Discernment

In our family, we listen to God's truth to understand how to live a righteous life for Him.

Ask: Discern which is better and why: breakfast, lunch, or dinner? *Star Wars* or *Star Trek*? Dogs or cats?

Read: Romans 12:2—And do not be conformed to this world, but be transformed by the renewing of your mind, so that you may prove what the will of God is, that which is good and acceptable and perfect.

Talk: Paul tells us to stop conforming to the time in which we live. How do we become conformed to what the world believes? How can we renew our minds? Where do we learn about the will of God so we can demonstrate that it is good?

SPEAK: Ask God for a discerning heart formed and shaped by His word in order to please Him and live a righteous life. Pray that your life will show the desirability of God's will.

Giving Words of GRACE

John 1:16–17—For of His fullness we have all received, and grace upon grace. For the Law was given through Moses; grace and truth were realized through Jesus Christ.

Word #5—Gift

In our family, we value all of God's generous and gracious gifts to us as His children.

ASK: If you had to give away one of your prized possessions, what would it be and who would you give it to?

READ: Hebrews 4:16—Therefore let us draw near with confidence to the throne of grace, so that we may receive mercy and find grace to help in time of need.

TALK: What do you think the throne of grace is? How can we draw near to it? Why can we have confidence to do that? What, exactly, are the mercy and grace that we'll receive and find there? How will those help us in a time of need?

SPEAK: Praise God for the fullness of life and grace upon grace we have received from Him. Thank God that you can confidently ask for His mercy and grace.

Word #6—Freedom

In our family, we live in the power of the Holy Spirit and by the freedom of God's grace.

Ask: It's "You Can Do Anything You Want To" day. What would you do?

Read: Romans 8:2—For the law of the Spirit of life in Christ Jesus has set you free from the law of sin and of death.

Talk: Paul has been teaching the Roman believers that they are no longer slaves to the Jewish law but are free in Christ. How is the "law of the Spirit" different from a written law? How does Christ's life in us set us free?

Speak: Pray that you will know and live every day in the freedom and power of the Holy Spirit. Thank God for the Spirit of life you have in Christ that sets you free.

Word #7—Redemption

In our family, we rejoice in our redemption from sin and in the redeeming grace of God.

Ask: Of all the broken and lost things you can imagine, what three things would you most want to rescue and redeem?

Read: Ephesians 1:7–8—In Him we have redemption through His blood, the forgiveness of our trespasses, according to the riches of His grace which He lavished on us.

Talk: To be redeemed means to be purchased out of slavery and set free. How did Christ's blood do that for us? How did our sins (trespasses) keep us enslaved? What are the "riches of [Christ's] grace" that are now ours?

Speak: Rejoice in your deliverance from sin and the redeeming power of grace. Praise God for the abundant riches of His grace that are now yours in Christ.

Word #8—Reconciliation

In our family, we rejoice that we are reconciled to our Creator by His love and grace.

ASK: You are "The Reconciler" superhero! What are your superpowers and what kind of super suit do you wear?

READ: Ephesians 2:8–9—For by grace you have been saved through faith; and that not of yourselves, it is the gift of God; not as a result of works, so that no one may boast.

TALK: Paul reminds the Ephesians that they were not saved by works, i.e., by works of the Law. Talk about each of the words Paul uses to describe how they were saved. How can those words prevent boasting of salvation?

SPEAK: Thank God that the love and grace of Christ has reconciled you to your Creator. Confess if you try to work for God's grace, and ask for help to just accept it in faith.

Giving Words of FAITH

Galatians 2:20—I have been crucified with Christ; and it is no longer I who live, but Christ lives in me; and the life which I now live in the flesh I live by faith in the Son of God, who loved me and gave Himself up for me.

Word #9—Trust

In our family, we walk by faith in Christ, trusting His love, loving His life, and living in His light.

ASK: Using a kind of balls as a rating ("4 tennis balls"), how much do you trust your dog? your best friend? your parents? a stranger? a pastor?

READ: Proverbs 3:5–6—Trust in the LORD with all your heart and do not lean on your own understanding. In all your ways acknowledge Him, and He will make your paths straight.

TALK: What all happens in the heart? How do you trust God with "all your heart"? How can you acknowledge God in "all your ways"? What is the advantage of a straight path? How does God make them straight?

SPEAK: Praise Jesus that you know Him and trust Him with your life, and you want to live by faith in His light. Acknowledge together your trust in God.

Word #10—Belief

In our family, we believe in our Lord, Jesus Christ, and in the words He gave and the work He did for us.

ASK: Other than your faith, what do you believe in so much that others would say you deserve a reward for it? What kind of reward?

READ: John 3:16–18—For God so loved the world, that He gave His only begotten Son, that whoever believes in Him shall not perish, but have eternal life. For God did not send the Son into the world to judge the world, but that the world might be saved through Him. He who believes in Him is not judged; he who does not believe has been judged already, because he has not believed in the name of the only begotten Son of God.

TALK: Jesus is explaining being born again. Is the world that God so loved just some people, or does God love all people? Why did He send Jesus into the world? What must anyone do to have eternal life? Believe what?

Speak: Thank the Lord for His truth, revealed in His word, and for His death on the cross for us. Confess together your belief in Jesus as God's Son and our Savior.

Word #11—Assurance

In our family, we live assured of God's salvation because of our faith in His sacrifice on the cross for us.

Ask: On a scale of one to ten, how confident are you that you can be anything you want to be in life? Why?

Read: Hebrews 11:1, 6—Now faith is the assurance of things hoped for, the conviction of things not seen. . . . And without faith it is impossible to please Him, for he who comes to God must believe that He is and that He is a rewarder of those who seek Him.

Talk: What is assurance (confidence of truth)? What is hope (trust in a possibility)? How can you be assured of something you hope for? Why does a lack of faith fail to please God? Can you have faith that God might be? Why not?

Speak: Thank the Lord for His loving offering of himself on our behalf on the cross. Say together the Apostles' Creed to affirm your belief in God and Christ.

Word #12—Endurance

In our family, we patiently endure whatever life brings, looking with faith to Jesus for help and hope.

Ask: Which endurance eating contests would you win— ice cream? salad? beans? pizza? zucchini? tacos? Skittles? What?

Read: James 1:2–4—Consider it all joy, my brethren, when you encounter various trials, knowing that the testing of your faith produces endurance. And let endurance have its perfect result, so that you may be perfect and complete, lacking in nothing.

TALK: What does it mean to consider something (ponder it as possible)? What kinds of trials would not be joyful? How do trials test your faith? How is endurance related to faith? How does endurance make us better?

SPEAK: Ask God to strengthen your faith to endure trials with grace and hope. Praise God that the joy of enduring trials is a closer and deeper walk with Him.

Giving Words of HOPE

Hebrews 6:19–20—This hope we have as an anchor of the soul, a hope both sure and steadfast and one which enters within the veil, where Jesus has entered as a forerunner for us, having become a high priest forever according to the order of Melchizedek.

Word #13—Promise

In our family, we believe the promises of God are our hope of an eternal relationship with Him.

ASK: Write a fun poem or song together about "Promises for Pronouns Like I, Me, You, and We."

READ: Romans 8:24–25—For in hope we have been saved, but hope that is seen is not hope; for who hopes for what he already sees? But if we hope for what we do not see, with perseverance we wait eagerly for it.

TALK: Hope is a belief (faith) in a future reality, such as our hope of salvation in Christ (saved from our sin). What

is a "hope that is seen" (a present reality)? What is the relationship between hope, perseverance, and waiting?
Speak: Praise God for the hope of salvation we have because of Jesus. Thank God that our hope is anchored in the person of Christ and in the cross.

Word #14—Purpose

In our family, we live with purpose, knowing that our hope is in God's loving and good work in our lives.

Ask: If your family were a business, what would your product or service be, and how could you be most successful?
Read: Romans 8:28—And we know that God causes all things to work together for good to those who love God, to those who are called according to His purpose.
Talk: Paul reminds us of our salvation that was secured by Christ. What does it say about God that He makes "all things work together for good" for those who love Him? What is the purpose for which we are called (salvation)?
Speak: Praise God for the purpose and meaning He brings to your life. Thank God that He is always at work for the good of those who love and follow Him.

Word #15—Kingdom

In our family, we hope for God's coming kingdom when Jesus will rule and reign over all creation.

Ask: If you were king of your neighborhood, what three "hoodidays" would you create and celebrate?
Read: 2 Peter 1:10–11—Therefore, brethren, be all the more diligent to make certain about His calling and choosing you; for as long as you practice these things, you will

never stumble; for in this way the entrance into the eternal kingdom of our Lord and Savior Jesus Christ will be abundantly supplied to you.

TALK: Peter has just finished describing godly virtues. How can one be diligent to confirm God's calling? How can practicing these virtues protect one from stumbling as a Christian? Why are they keys into Christ's eternal kingdom?

SPEAK: Acknowledge together that Christ is Lord and King of your life. Thank God that you can be certain of your entrance into Christ's eternal kingdom.

Word #16—Gospel

In our family, we hope in the good news that God loved us, Jesus died for us, and the Spirit gives us new life.

ASK: You're the editor of the *Our Family Good News Gazette*. What are the headlines for this week?

READ: Colossians 1:22–23—Yet He has now reconciled you in His fleshly body through death, in order to present you before Him holy and blameless and beyond reproach—if indeed you continue in the faith firmly established and steadfast, and not moved away from the hope of the gospel that you have heard, which was proclaimed in all creation under heaven, and of which I, Paul, was made a minister.

TALK: How did Christ reconcile us to God (restore our broken relationship)? What does Paul say a faith that is firm and steadfast looks like? What is our "hope of the gospel" (to be "holy and blameless and beyond reproach")?

SPEAK: Praise God for the gospel, the good news that Christ died on the cross for your sins. Thank God for the new life you have in Him because of the gospel.

Giving Words of LOVE

First John 4:7–8—Beloved, let us love one another, for love is from God; and everyone who loves is born of God and knows God. The one who does not love does not know God, for God is love.

Word #17—Acceptance

In our family, we love one another with unconditional acceptance because that is how God loves us.

ASK: *Different* is another word for *unique*. What "different" things about you do you want others to say are special?
READ: 1 Corinthians 13:4–7—Love is patient, love is kind and is not jealous; love does not brag and is not arrogant, does not act unbecomingly; it does not seek its own, is not provoked, does not take into account a wrong suffered, does not rejoice in unrighteousness, but rejoices with the truth; bears all things, believes all things, hopes all things, endures all things.
TALK: This is about loving like God loves. Make a list of the things that love is and that love is not. What are the most difficult qualities of love to practice? What are the easiest? Does Paul really mean "all things" or just most things?
SPEAK: Pray that your family will love one another with the love that God has for each of you. Pray that the Spirit of God will work in you the true love of God.

Word #18—Encouragement

In our family, we encourage one another, stimulating one another to love and good deeds.

240

Ask: Make this "Say It Forward" day. Whenever you're encouraged, you encourage someone else. You're awesome! Start now.

Read: Hebrews 10:23–25—Let us hold fast the confession of our hope without wavering, for He who promised is faithful; and let us consider how to stimulate one another to love and good deeds, not forsaking our own assembling together, as is the habit of some, but encouraging one another; and all the more as you see the day drawing near.

Talk: Why does our hope that is secure motivate us to action? We know we must love and do good to others, but what more does the writer suggest? How can we stimulate one another that way? What does encouragement do for us?

Speak: Ask God to give you scriptures and words to encourage others in the Lord. Pray that your family will encourage one another with love and good deeds.

Word #19—Kindness

In our family, we are kind and merciful to others because of God's love, kindness, and mercy for us.

Ask: Play the "I Spy Kindness" game today. Talk about all the different acts of kindness you've seen and done.

Read: Colossians 3:12–14—So, as those who have been chosen of God, holy and beloved, put on a heart of compassion, kindness, humility, gentleness and patience; bearing with one another, and forgiving each other, whoever has a complaint against anyone; just as the Lord forgave you, so also should you. Beyond all these things put on love, which is the perfect bond of unity.

TALK: Because we are loved by God, Paul encourages us to wear the character of Christ like a garment. How do you "put on a heart" of godly character? What qualities stand out to you? How important is kindness for a heart of love?

SPEAK: Thank God for the kindness of His love and mercy that He has shown to you, His child. Pray that you can show that same love and kindness to others.

Word #20—Gentleness

In our family, we express our love by being gentle with one another as a fruit of the Holy Spirit.

ASK: If you were entrusted with an egg today, how would you care for it so it would not get broken? Describe your egg carrier.

READ: 1 Peter 3:15—But sanctify Christ as Lord in your hearts, always being ready to make a defense to everyone who asks you to give an account for the hope that is in you, yet with gentleness and reverence.

TALK: Gentleness is a fruit of the Holy Spirit and a quality of Christ's character. How do we sanctify (set apart as holy) Christ in our hearts? Why are gentleness and reverence necessary for telling others about our hope in Christ?

SPEAK: Pray for the fruit of the Spirit in your life, that you will have a spirit of gentleness toward your family. Pray for gentleness in your witness to others.

Giving Words of LIFE

John 10:10—The thief comes only to steal and kill and destroy; I came that they may have life, and have it abundantly.

242

Word #21—Joy

In our family, we rejoice with God in this life and in the life to come because of Christ, our Savior.

ASK: Make up new words that describe a special joyfulness—icecreameating, happitea, joyosity.

READ: 1 Peter 1:8–9—And though you have not seen Him, you love Him, and though you do not see Him now, but believe in Him, you greatly rejoice with joy inexpressible and full of glory, obtaining as the outcome of your faith the salvation of your souls.

TALK: Joy is a fruit of the Holy Spirit and a quality of Christ's character within our hearts. Why do we love and believe in Christ even though we have not seen Him? Why does our faith in Him make us "rejoice with joy inexpressible"?

SPEAK: Praise and thank God for the life you have in Christ and the joy that brings to your spirit. Rejoice together as a family for your salvation in Christ.

Word #22—Peace

In our family, we know that God's peace will guard our hearts and minds in all circumstances of life.

ASK: You must guard the kingdom's "Peace Well" from the invading Troublelanders! What do you do to keep the peace?

READ: Romans 8:6—For the mind set on the flesh is death, but the mind set on the Spirit is life and peace.

TALK: Peace is a fruit of the Holy Spirit and a quality of Christ's character within our hearts. What does it mean to have a "mind set on the flesh" (sin) or "set on the Spirit" (righteousness)? How does the Spirit give us life and peace?

SPEAK: Pray for the peace of God, the fruit of His Spirit, to guard your family's hearts and minds. Ask for the Spirit to help you set your mind on Him today.

Word #23—Goodness

In our family, we live expecting that the grace and goodness of God will sustain and bless our lives.

ASK: Looking back as a family, talk about some difficulties and trials from which good has come by God's hand.
READ: Psalm 31:19—How great is Your goodness, which You have stored up for those who fear You, which You have wrought for those who take refuge in You, before the sons of men!
TALK: The psalmist praises God for His eternal goodness. How might God store up goodness for those who fear Him? How has He wrought (worked) goodness for those who take refuge in Him? When do we need God's goodness most?
SPEAK: Praise God for His loving, life-sustaining goodness toward you. Thank God for the blessings of His goodness that you enjoy personally and as a family.

Word #24—Spirit

In our family, we live every day in the power of the Holy Spirit, who gives us Christ's life for this life.

ASK: The Holy Spirit is a person of the trinity. If the Spirit were seated at your table, what things would you ask and talk about?
READ: Romans 8:10–11—If Christ is in you, though the body is dead because of sin, yet the spirit is alive because

of righteousness. But if the Spirit of Him who raised Jesus from the dead dwells in you, He who raised Christ Jesus from the dead will also give life to your mortal bodies through His Spirit who dwells in you.

TALK: Our life in Christ is our life in the Spirit. Why is an otherwise living body dead "because of sin"? Why is our spirit alive "because of righteousness"? What does it mean that Jesus, who rose from the dead, lives in us and gives us life?

SPEAK: Thank God that He has given you His Spirit, who enables you to live a life pleasing to God. Pray for the lifegiving work of the Spirit who dwells in you.

Notes

Introduction

1. Plutarch (c. AD 50–120), Greek philosopher and historian, from the essay "On Listening to Lectures."

2. Anti-drug campaign by *Partnership for a Drug-Free America* (PDFA), TV PSA launched in 1987 by the Ad Council.

Chapter 1 In the Beginning Was the Words

1. N. T. Wright, *Scripture and the Authority of God* (New York: HarperCollins, 2013), 36–37.

2. Augustine, *City of God*, Book XI, chapter 7.

3. C. S. Lewis, *The Magician's Nephew* (New York: Harper-Collins, 2000), 126.

4. *The Encyclopedia of the Bible*, Word of the Lord, https://www.biblegateway.com/resources/encyclopedia-of-the-bible/Word-Lord.

Chapter 2 The Words You Say

1. C. S. Lewis, *The Weight of Glory and Other Addresses* (New York: Macmillan Publishing Company, 1980), 16.

Chapter 3 Saying the Words

1. George MacDonald, quoted in Edward Porter St. John, *Stories and Story-Telling in Moral and Religious Education* (Boston: The Pilgrim Press, 1910), 21, public domain.

2. "Screen Time and Children," American Academy of Child and Adolescent Psychiatry, 54, 2020, www.aacap.org/AACAP/Families_and_Youth/Facts_for_Families/FFF-Guide/Children-And-Watching-TV-054.aspx.

3. Ben Renner, "Modern Family: Average Parent Spends Just 5 Hours Face-To-Face with Their Kids Per Week!" Study Finds, January 25, 2020, www.studyfinds.org

/modern-family-average-parent
-spends-just-5-hours-face-to-face
-with-their-kids-per-week.

4. "Adult-Child Conversations
Strengthen Language Regions of
Developing Brain," NeuroscienceNews.com, August 13, 2018,
https://neurosciencenews.com/lan
guage-adult-child-9698.

5. Dr. Holly Ordway, "Practice,
Patience, Prayer: Lessons in Evangelization from the Parables," July
19, 2021, Word on Fire Catholic
Ministries, www.wordonfire.org
/articles/fellows/practice-patience
-prayer-lessons-in-evangelization
-from-the-parables.

6. Albert Mehrabian, Professor
Emeritus of Psychology at UCLA,
postulated from his research of
body language in the 1970s that
face-to-face communication is
55 percent nonverbal, 38 percent
vocal, and 7 percent words, all
popularly expressed as 90 percent
nonverbal. Jeff Thompson, PhD,
"Is Nonverbal Communication
a Numbers Game?" *Psychology
Today*, September 30, 2011, www
.psychologytoday.com/us/blog/be
yond-words/201109/is-nonverbal
-communication-numbers-game.

7. Louise Seymour Houghton
(1838–1920, Christian author in
Victorian England), quoted in
Edward Porter St. John, *Stories
and Story-Telling in Moral and
Religious Education* (Boston: The
Pilgrim Press, 1910), 21, public
domain.

8. Pioneering psychologist
and educator G. Stanley Hall
(1844–1924), first president of the

American Psychological Association, leader in the "child-study"
movement, quoted in *Stories and
Story-Telling*, 102.

9. "Good Questions Should
Be" and "Good Questions Should
Not Be" are adapted from Clay
Clarkson with Sally Clarkson, *Educating the WholeHearted Child*
(Monument, CO: Whole Heart
Press, 2019), 242.

10. Note: Bulleted list for
family storytelling suggestions
adapted from Clay Clarkson with
Sally Clarkson, *Educating the
WholeHearted Child*, 241.

11. Brian Godawa, *Word Pictures* (Downers Grove, IL: InterVarsity, 2009), 72.

12. Madeleine L'Engle, *Walking on Water* (Colorado Springs:
WaterBrook, 1980, 1998, 2001),
36.

Chapter 4 Words That Are Personal

1. C. S. Lewis, *Till We Have
Faces: A Myth Retold* (London:
Harcourt, 1956), 294.

Chapter 5 Words That Are Loving

1. Mary Elizabeth Dallas, "Eating Feeds 'Feel Good' Hormones
in the Brain," WebMD.com, August 31, 2017, www.webmd.com
/brain/news/20170831/eating-feeds
-feel-good-hormones-in-the-brain.

2. Ross Campbell, MD, *Relational Parenting* (Chicago: Moody
Press, 2000), 40.

3. Dr. Tim Kimmel, *Grace-Based Parenting* (Nashville: W Publishing Group, 2004), 52.

Chapter 6 Words That Are Nurturing

1. Tim Kimmel, *Grace-Based Parenting*, 19.
2. C. S. Lewis, "Meditation in a Toolshed" in *God in the Dock* (Grand Rapids, MI: Eerdmans, 1998), 212–215.
3. Gary Smalley and John Trent, PhD, *The Blessing* (Nashville, TN: Thomas Nelson, 1986), 49–50.

Chapter 7 Words That Are Spiritual

1. Henry David Thoreau, *The Journal, 1837–1861* (New York: The New York Review of Books, 2009), 65.
2. Sarah Clarkson, *Book Girl* (Carol Stream, IL: Tyndale, 2018), 136.
3. Madeleine L'Engle, *Walking on Water: Reflections on Life and Art* (WaterBrook Press, Crosswicks Ltd. 1980, 1998, 2001), 53.

Chapter 8 Words That Are Wisdom

1. Eugene H. Peterson, *The Jesus Way* (Grand Rapids, MI: Eerdmans, 2007), 40.
2. Lawrence O. Richards, *The New International Encyclopedia of Bible Words* (Grand Rapids, MI: Zondervan, 1985, 1991), 630.

Chapter 9 Words That Are Believable

1. For more on childhood faith, see *The Lifegiving Parent* (Tyndale, 2018), chapter 6; *Heartfelt Discipline* (Whole Heart Press, 2014), chapter 2; and *Educating the WholeHearted Child* (Whole Heart Press, 2019), chapter 3.
2. Rex Rouis, "Faith/Believe— Most Frequently Used New Testament Words," HopeFaithPrayer, www.hopefaithprayer.com/inter esting-word-occurrences.
3. Andrew Murray, *Raising Your Child to Love God* (Minneapolis: Bethany House, 1975, 2001), 263–264.
4. N. T. Wright, *Surprised by Hope* (New York: HarperOne, 2008), 251.
5. Glenn R. Paauw, *Saving the Bible from Ourselves* (Downers Grove, IL: InterVarsity Press, 2016), 110.
6. N. T. Wright, *The New Testament and the People of God* (Minneapolis: Fortress, 1992), 6.
7. H. Clay Trumbull, *Hints on Child-Training* (Philadelphia: John D. Wattles, 1890), 129, public domain.
8. Andrew Murray, *Raising Your Child to Love God* (Bethany House, 1975, 2001), 265.

Epilogue

1. C. S. Lewis, *The Weight of Glory* (New York: HarperCollins, 2001), 46.

About the Authors

Sally Clarkson is the mother of four wholehearted children, an inspirational conference speaker for more than twenty-five years, and a champion of biblical motherhood. She has inspired thousands of women through her SallyClarkson. com blog since 2007, and her *At Home with Sally* podcast has been downloaded millions of times. She also encourages women through her LifewithSally.com membership community and Mom Heart Ministry small groups. She is a bestselling author with over twenty books on motherhood, parenting, and Christian living, including *The Mission of Motherhood*, *Own Your Life*, *The Lifegiving Home* (with Sarah Clarkson), *Different* (with Nathan Clarkson), *Mom Heart Moments*, *Awaking Wonder*, and *Help, I'm Drowning*. Sally loves the companionship of her family, thoughtful books, beautiful music, regular tea times, candlelight, walking, and being with her children and grandchildren.

Clay Clarkson is the executive director of Whole Heart Ministries, the nonprofit Christian home and parenting ministry he and Sally founded in 1994. He has coordinated countless church workshops and over sixty ministry conferences. He has written or cowritten numerous books, including *Educating the WholeHearted Child*, *Our 24 Family Ways*, *Heartfelt Discipline*, and *The Lifegiving Parent*. He also conceives, develops, and writes books published by Whole Heart Press. Clay earned a master of divinity degree with honors from Denver Seminary in 1985 and ministered on church staffs overseas and in the States before starting Whole Heart Ministries. He is also a songwriter and sometimes singer, occasional poet, and inconsistent blogger (he resides online at ClayClarkson.com). After living in nineteen homes in three countries and four states, Clay and Sally have made their home in Monument, Colorado, in the shadow of Pikes Peak, since 2005.

— • —

For information about everyone in the Clarkson family, visit **ClarksonFamily.com**, where you'll find full profiles, links to projects and websites, and bibliographies.

Clarkson Family Words

All Clarkson family parents and children are words people, and all are authors. Below is a bibliography of books they have written, along with other verbal efforts.

SALLY CLARKSON

Help, I'm Drowning

Awaking Wonder

Awaking Wonder Experience (with Clay)

Educating the WholeHearted Child (with Clay)

Only You Can Be You (with Nathan)

Mom Heart Moments

Girls' Club (with Sarah, Joy)

Girls' Club Experience (with Sarah, Joy)

The Lifegiving Parent (with Clay)

The Lifegiving Parent Experience (with Clay)

The Lifegiving Table

The Lifegiving Table Experience (with Joel, Joy)

The Lifegiving Home (with Sarah)

The Lifegiving Home Experience (with Joel)

Different (with Nathan)

A Different Kind of Hero
(with Joel)

Own Your Life

Own Your Life Experience
(with Joy)

Desperate (with Sarah Mae)

You Are Loved
(with Angela Perritt)

10 Gifts of Heart

Taking Motherhood to Hearts
(with Clay)

Your Mom Walk with God

*Dancing with My Heavenly
Father*

The Ministry of Motherhood

The Mission of Motherhood

Seasons of a Mother's Heart

Also: blog, podcast

CLAY CLARKSON

Awaking Wonder Experience
(with Sally)

The Lifegiving Parent
(with Sally)

*The Lifegiving Parent
Experience* (with Sally)

Taking Motherhood to Hearts
(with Sally)

Heartfelt Discipline

*Our 24 Family Ways:
Family Devotional Guide*

*Our 24 Family Ways:
Kids Color-In Book*

*Educating the WholeHearted
Child* (with Sally)

SARAH CLARKSON

This Beautiful Truth

Book Girl

Girls' Club (with Sally, Joy)

The Lifegiving Home
(with Sally)

Caught Up in a Story

Read for the Heart

Journeys of Faithfulness

Also: blog, podcast, Patreon

JOEL CLARKSON

Sensing God

A Different Kind of Hero
(with Sally)

The Lifegiving Table Experience (with Sally, Joy)

The Lifegiving Home Experience (with Sally)

Also: piano albums, choral compositions, audiobooks

NATHAN CLARKSON

The Way of Kings

The Clubhouse (with Joy)

Good Man

Only You Can Be You
(with Sally)

Different (with Sally)

Wisdom Chasers

Also: screenwriting, filmmaking, blog, podcast

JOY CLARKSON

Aggressively Happy

The Clubhouse (with Nathan)

Girls' Club (with Sally, Sarah)

The Lifegiving Table Experience (with Sally, Joel)

Own Your Life Experience
(with Sally)

Also: blog, podcast, Patreon

SALLY CLARKSON

AUTHOR | SPEAKER | LIFEGIVER

Beloved author and speaker Sally Clarkson has dedicated her life to the art of mentoring women, encouraging mothers, and educating children. If you would like more daily encouragement in your life from Sally, visit her online at these websites and pages:

Website & Blog | **SallyClarkson.com**
Find daily encouragement for your journey as a woman, mom, and believer on Sally's blog as she shares thoughts, insights, inspiration, wisdom, recipes, traditions, and prayers. You can also stay up to date with her speaking schedule, events, and conferences.

Online Community | **LifewithSally.com**
Life with Sally is an online community of women that was created to reach, teach, and mentor moms worldwide in a more personal way. It is filled with Sally's talks, videos, recipes, Bible studies, workbooks, a forum, and more. It is an online resource to invite a bit of community, wisdom, and joy into today's women's worlds.

Podcast Page | **AtHomewithSally.com**
Sally invites you into her home and shares personal stories, spiritual insight, and hard-earned wisdom about being a woman, mom, and believer. Filled with dynamic and relevant guests, this podcast, which has been downloaded more than eight million times, will give you a personal and intimate connection into Sally's heart, mind, and home.

Social Media
Facebook | **@TheRealSallyClarkson**
Instagram | **@Sally.Clarkson**
Twitter | **Sally_Clarkson**

WHOLE HEART MINISTRIES

KEEPING FAITH IN THE FAMILY

Whole Heart Ministries is a nonprofit Christian home and parenting ministry founded by Clay and Sally Clarkson in 1994. From the beginning, our mission has been to give help and hope to Christian parents to raise wholehearted children for Christ. Our current strategic ministry initiatives include Sally Clarkson Ministry, Mom Heart Ministry, Storyformed Project, Family Faith Project, Lifegiving Family Project, and WholeHearted Learning. We are keeping faith in the family.

Whole Heart Ministries
PO Box 3445 | Monument, CO 80132
719-488-4466 | 888-488-4466
whm@wholeheart.org | admin@wholeheart.org

For more information, visit our ministry website:
WholeHeart.org

More from Sally Clarkson

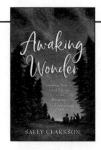

In our outcome-based, technologically driven society, it is easy to lose sight of the innocence and uniqueness of each child. In these pages, Sally Clarkson helps parents unearth the hidden potential of their child's imagination, learning capacity, and ability to engage authentically with the world using the same principles that guided her.

Awaking Wonder

In the midst of a storm, it's easy to feel lonely, exhausted, fearful, and helpless. In these pages, Sally Clarkson helps you to find your anchors for life's storms. She will encourage you to combat loneliness with intentional engagement and community, find healing and forgiveness, embrace God's strength as the determiner of your battles, and more.

Help, I'm Drowning

◊ BETHANYHOUSE

Stay up to date on your favorite books and authors with our free e-newsletters. Sign up today at bethanyhouse.com.

 facebook.com/BHPnonfiction

 @bethany_house

 @bethany_house_nonfiction